T0301606

U.S. Insurance Regulation

For Rise, who encouraged me to pursue my passions and follow my dreams

U.S. Insurance Regulation
A Primer

Richard G. Liskov

Senior Counsel, ArentFox Schiff LLP and Lecturer, School of Law, Boston University, USA

Edward Elgar
PUBLISHING

Cheltenham, UK • Northampton, MA, USA

Cover image: Susan Gold on Unsplash

Published by
Edward Elgar Publishing Limited
The Lypiatts
15 Lansdown Road
Cheltenham
Glos GL50 2JA
UK

Edward Elgar Publishing, Inc.
William Pratt House
9 Dewey Court
Northampton
Massachusetts 01060
USA

A catalogue record for this book
is available from the British Library

Library of Congress Control Number: 2023945139

This book is available electronically in the **Elgar**online
Law subject collection
http://dx.doi.org/10.4337/9781035314799

ISBN 978 1 0353 1478 2 (cased)
ISBN 978 1 0353 1479 9 (eBook)

Printed and bound by CPI Group (UK) Ltd, Croydon, CR0 4YY

Contents

Acknowledgements

To the extent this book reflects my expertise in U.S. insurance regulation, I could not have written it had I not gained valuable insights in government and insurance from numerous colleagues at the major law firms in which I practiced, including John J. Sarchio, Esq. with whom I collaborated on insurance regulatory matters for over twenty-five years. Four former dedicated public servants enabled and furthered my training in the subject: Robert Abrams, elected four times as Attorney General of the State of New York, who in 1980 appointed me an Assistant Attorney General tasked with representing the New York State Insurance Department in state and federal courts; James P. Corcoran, one of the longest serving Superintendents of Insurance of the State of New York; Salvatore Curiale, Superintendent of Insurance, both of whom I was honored to serve as Deputy Superintendent and General Counsel of the New York State Insurance Department between 1989 and 1992; and, Wendy Cooper, Acting Superintendent of Insurance and previously First Deputy Superintendent of Insurance, from whom I learned much about how government worked effectively.

Since 2019 I have been privileged to teach online in the Financial Services Compliance Certificate Program at the School of Law of Boston University. My thanks to Mary Moran Zeven, former Director, Graduate Program in Banking and Financial Law, and Lorraine Kaplan, Associate Director of Graduate and Online Programs, for recommending my appointment and helping me with the course. The information in this work is derived from my teaching materials.

In helping me edit this book I am grateful to Barbara McDonald, Legal Secretary, and Akili T. Kumasi, Document Analyst, at ArentFox Schiff LLP; and, in offering invaluable editorial suggestions Monica R. Jacobson, Esq., who served with me at the Office of the Attorney General of the State of New York, and Francis L. McGrath, who ably assisted my practice as a very knowledgeable legal assistant at several major firms, including White & Case and Holland & Knight.

Finally, throughout the writing process I have been exceedingly thankful for the love and support of my sons, Alan, David and Aaron and my daughter-in-law, Tina Wang.

AUTHOR'S NOTE

The statements made by the author are personal to him, and do not purport to be, and should not be deemed to be, the statements of ArentFox Schiff or any of its clients.

New York
May, 2023

1. An overview of U.S. insurance regulation and some key definitions

I. WHAT THIS PRIMER WILL COVER

This primer is not an exhaustive treatise and is intended to provide an overview of insurance regulation in the United States. The book is written for non-experts and contains in Chapters 2 and 3 a discussion of the respective roles of the federal government and U.S. states for regulating insurance. It will next discuss in Chapter 4 how U.S. states license insurance companies, insurance agents, brokers, producers, and other insurance professionals, such as adjusters, who deal with consumers, and how states permit unlicensed insurers to underwrite coverage on risks that licensed insurers will not cover.

Chapter 5 explains how state insurance departments monitor the financial health of licensed insurers, using such tools as periodic financial reports and examinations. Chapter 6 discusses how those departments handle insurers in financial distress through state court proceedings called rehabilitations and liquidations.

Chapter 7 analyzes how state insurance departments in the U.S. regulate the market conduct of insurance companies and other licensees, including fair claims handling, as well as, how truthful and complete are advertisements for insurance coverage, how fairly and accurately do insurers underwrite their policies—deciding whether to insure, for how much, and on what terms, and whether the rates which insurance companies charge for coverage are excessive, inadequate or unfairly discriminatory.

In addition, the book will address the following topics:

- health insurance—the one area in which the federal government plays a leading regulatory role (Chapter 8); and
- what trends are emerging in international insurance regulation affecting U.S. insurance companies; and

- how U.S. state insurance regulators are grappling with the increasing importance of technology in insurance, e.g. cyberinsurance, drones, blockchain, artificial intelligence/machine learning, and telematics. (Chapter 9)

Please note that every statement you will read in this book represents my own analysis of relevant laws and governmental policies. None of the statements you read in this book purport to be, or should be deemed as, the views of any of the law firms in which I practiced or of any client of any of those law firms.

II.   WHY INSURANCE IS REGULATED

Governments throughout the world, including the federal government and the individual states in the U.S., regulate the business of insurance for several reasons. First, from an economic standpoint, insurance is a key component of modern, functioning economies, and without reliable coverage underwritten by companies that will endure, many crucial activities—driving, manufacturing, construction, housing, lending, among others—would quickly grind to a halt, throwing society suddenly back into a pre-industrial miasma. Second, many governments have considered it imperative to protect constituents in their role as consumers, so insurance regulation has increasingly focused on the market conduct of insurance companies—e.g. life and accident insurers, property/casualty insurers, title and mortgage guaranty insurers, health insurers—and insurance professionals, such as agents, brokers and adjusters. In this role regulators strive to enforce rules that prohibit unfair and deceptive practices in the underwriting and sale of insurance policies which, with their exclusions, deductibles, co-pays, limits, and sometimes sub-limits, and often legalistic language, can be confusing and complicated for ordinary consumers. Third, as to health insurance, the U.S. does not have, on a national basis, a single-payer system for citizens of all ages, such as the National Health Service in the United Kingdom (U.K.). Therefore, U.S. presidents and members of Congress have considered it essential to establish and maintain a regulated private health insurance regime that combines certain national standards for coverage—including health insurance which covers retirees under their employer's pension and welfare plans—in conjunction with additional protections required by individual U.S. states.

In fashioning sound insurance regulation, governmental officials in the U.S. aim to satisfy two overriding objectives of equal importance: (i) ensuring that licensed insurance companies are financially healthy and sufficiently profitable to stay in business, and (ii) ensuring that those companies and the professionals who work with them operate with fairness, reasonableness, honesty, and competence to benefit policyholders, claimants, and creditors, as well as the public generally. Sometimes tension between these two overarching aims is evident, as, for example, when U.S. state insurance regulators must decide if a proposed increase in an insurance company's premium rates is justified. Although as human beings insurance regulators do make mistakes and, in relatively rare instances have been convicted of crimes such as bribery, it has been the author's experience over more than forty years that U.S. insurance regulators almost always seek to do the right thing in as fair, thoughtful and transparent a way as possible.

III.　SOME BASIC REGULATORY TERMINOLOGY

To fully understand how insurance is regulated in the U.S. it is first necessary to know some key terms. We will start with some basic regulatory terms, two of which are: "direct insurer" and "admitted". A person is covered by a direct insurer for one or more specified risks—e.g. certainly sickness, possibly death, and liability for another person's injury or death in an automobile accident. An insurance company, such as a health insurer, is "*admitted*"—i.e. licensed or authorized by the state in which the covered person and any dependents obtained the policy. Some insurers can be both direct insurers, dealing directly with policyholders and claimants, as well as reinsurers which sell reinsurance to direct insurers.

Other important terms are "domestic" and "ancillary". The U.S. state in which an insurance company is domiciled—where it is incorporated—is the "*domestic*" state. All of the other states in which the company is admitted are "*ancillary*" states. Insurers must comply with rules in both the domestic state *and* all ancillary states, but, as we shall see, the domestic state regulates the insurer most stringently in terms of overseeing its formation and monitoring its solvency

Insurance companies licensed in one or more U.S. states, but domiciled in another state, are called "*foreign*" insurers, even though they operate only inside the U.S. An insurance company domiciled outside of the U.S., say in the U.K., but which is authorized to operate in the U.S.

by one or more states is an "*alien*" insurer. We shall consider the special requirements applicable to authorized alien insurers in Chapter 4.

As we shall also see in Chapter 4, not all insurers are required to be licensed in a state in order to transact insurance there legally. Lloyds is the most prominent example of an unlicensed insurer which legally covers risks throughout the U.S. every day. These legal, albeit unlicensed, insurers operate in what is termed the "*surplus line*" or "*excess line*" market, dealing with specially licensed "*surplus line brokers*" or "*excess line brokers*". (The terms "surplus" and "excess" in this context are interchangeable and mean the same.) These surplus line or excess line brokers, who must be licensed in the states in which they do business, are permitted to place coverage with unlicensed insurers under certain specified conditions, typically when admitted insurers do not wish to cover an unusual risk, such as liability for operating an amusement park, or do not wish to cover as much of the risk as a policyholder wants. States do not directly regulate unlicensed surplus line or excess line insurers, but they do prescribe the particular requirements which the specially licensed "surplus line brokers" must meet in order to place business with surplus line or excess line insurers. Even the U.S. Congress has enacted uniform rules for the surplus line or excess line market as we will see in that chapter.

A direct life or property insurer may well have bought its own insurance from a *reinsurer* for all or part of the risk it agreed to cover to the policyholder and additional insureds, if any, or a beneficiary of a life insurance policy. Many leading reinsurers are non-U.S. companies—e.g. Munich Re, Swiss Re, and Lloyds syndicates. In turn, a reinsurer typically wants insurance for its own liabilities to the direct insurer, so it buys reinsurance from a *retrocessionaire* for all or part of its liabilities.

In the world of reinsurance, two key terms are: "*Cede*" and "*assume*". A direct insurer agrees to *cede* all or part of the risk—say, 60 percent of each loss—to the reinsurer who agrees to *assume* that risk, i.e. has agreed to cover the liability of the direct insurer for that specified percentage. Some reinsurance contracts provide that the reinsurer shall be liable for a specified amount on each covered policy—an amount exceeding, say, $1 million, on each policy. That reinsurer may have insured part of its own liability to the direct insurer by buying reinsurance of its own from a *retrocessionaire*, ceding that part of the risk, say, 20 percent of all losses over $10 million, to a *retrocessionaire* which assumes it. As discussed in Chapter 5, states do not regulate reinsurers and *retrocessionaires* which are usually not licensed, but they do insist that licensed direct insurers obtain collateral from some unlicensed reinsurers—mainly those domiciled outside of the U.K. and European Union (EU)—to ensure that policyholders and claimants are paid on valid claims.

State regulators often speak of two basic kinds of insurers, depending on how they are organized: "*stock*" insurers and "*mutual*" insurers. A *stock insurer* is a corporation with one or more classes of stockholders with common and sometimes preferred shares. The shareholders elect the directors, and if certain conditions are met, receive dividends on their stock. The shareholders need not be policyholders, and usually they are not. A *mutual insurer* does not issue stock; the policyholders are the owners; they elect directors, and—if certain specified conditions are met—receive dividends on their policies. If the policies are assessable, the policyholders can be charged assessments to help pay for the losses of other policyholders. Some of the most well-known life insurance companies in the U.S. are mutual insurers which issue non-assessable life insurance policies and annuity contracts.

Insurance is typically sold through a "*producer*", i.e. an insurance *agent* or *broker* who arranges the purchase of direct insurance. Some states distinguish between agents and brokers, while others call all of them "*producers*". *A producer acting on behalf of a direct insurer is an agent* who must be appointed by that insurer. Some agents are "captive" agents—they deal only on behalf of one insurer or affiliated group of insurers—e.g. State Farm Insurance Company agents. *A producer acting on behalf of a prospective policyholder is a broker.* Some producers can act both as agents and brokers depending on whether an insurance company has appointed them as agents. Some states like New York have separate licenses for agents and brokers; other states like Florida have one producer license covering both. As we shall see in Chapter 4, every state requires an insurance broker, or an insurance agent, or an insurance producer, to be licensed.

A "*managing general agent*" is an agent, appointed by a licensed insurer" to handle all or part of the insurer's business by deciding whether to underwrite the insurance on a particular risk, deciding the rates for such insurance subject to applicable state laws, and interacting with the retail agents who actually deal with the prospective policyholders. Each managing general agent must be licensed in each state in which she or he operates. States also require each *reinsurance intermediary*, who represents a reinsurer selling reinsurance or a direct insurer buying reinsurance, to be licensed. These various licensing requirements are discussed in Chapter 4.

IV.   SOME BASIC INSURANCE ACCOUNTING TERMINOLOGY

Every day insurance companies, and U.S. insurance regulators, consider some key insurance accounting terms. One of these is "*loss ratio*"—the proportion of each premium dollar allocated to paying losses, *and* expenses allocated to specific losses called "*Loss adjustment expenses*" such as attorneys' fees on particular claims. Another important metric is an insurance company's "*expense ratio*"—the proportion of each premium dollar allocated to general, unallocated expenses, e.g. rent, debt service, salaries of personnel at the insurer, IT systems, and taxes—all items not associated with particular claims but which are part of general overhead. An insurance company's "*combined ratio*" is the sum of incurred losses and allocated and unallocated expenses divided by earned premium:

Losses + Expenses (divided by)
Earned Premium

"*Earned premium*" is the amount of premium on a particular policy which the insurer is permitted to retain because it was on the risk for a specified length of time which has elapsed. In the U.S., for example, automobile insurance is frequently paid for in six-month installments. If the policy is cancelled after three months, the insurer has only "earned" three months of premium, and the remaining three months premium is considered "unearned" and must be returned to the policyholder (or the premium finance company if the premiums were financed), less a permissible administrative fee which is set by applicable state law.

An insurer with a combined ratio of more than 100 percent is paying out more in losses and expenses than it is receiving in premiums. Nevertheless, that insurer can still be profitable and continue in business *if* its investments return sufficient investment income so that the insurer is generating a "*Policyholder surplus*". The insurer and its regulators measure its "policyholder surplus" as the difference between its admitted assets and all of its liabilities, including its overhead and various reserves. Three important types of reserves are: (1) the insurance company's "*Unearned premium reserve*" to pay back unearned premium, (2) its "*case reserves*" for losses and associated "loss adjustment expenses", such as, for example, attorney's fees to defend policyholders sued for various torts, on claims already reported to the insurer; and, (3) an

"*IBNR*" ("incurred but not reported") reserve for losses the insurer reasonably knows it has incurred but which have not yet been formally noticed to it. Billions of dollars of pollution and asbestos claims have had to be reported by numerous insurance companies since the 1970s as IBNR reserves, and some insurance companies were determined to have a "*negative surplus*", i.e. a deficiency, with liabilities exceeding assets, because of their huge IBNR exposures.

As we shall see in Chapter 5, U.S. states regulate what kind of investments a licensed insurer may make and how much of the insurer's assets can be invested in particular investments, such as stocks, bonds, U.S. Treasury bills, real estate that the insurer uses for its own offices and which it can lease to others, real estate mortgages which it issues to commercial borrowers, and investments in non-U.S. companies. Permissible investments are deemed "*admitted assets*"; investments that are non-compliant are called "*Non-admitted assets*", and states such as New York, disallow the value of "non-admitted assets" in calculating "policyholder surplus".

Insurance companies are required to use "*statutory accounting principles*" (SAP) for the annual and quarterly financial statements which states require all licensed companies to file. By contrast, the insurer's parent company, if there is one, and its non-insurer affiliates, if there are any, are allowed to file GAAP financial statements, utilizing Generally Accepted Accounting Principles, as permitted by the Securities & Exchange Commission for public companies, and by various professional accounting organizations. In general, as discussed in Chapter 5, SAP is a more conservative accounting method with no allowance for goodwill or "going concern value". Rather, the insurer's use of SAP for its financial statements is intended to provide a snapshot of the company's finances as of the specified "as of" date, and its ability to pay valid claims and associated loss adjustment expenses as of that date—as if the insurer had ceased all operations on that date.

In that way regulators can tell how much policyholder surplus the insurer retains, whether there is a "*deficiency*", and whether the insurer is "*impaired*" financially for which various remedial steps must be taken, which we will cover in Chapter 6. At worst, an insurer may become "*insolvent*" with its liabilities exceeding its admitted assets, such that "*rehabilitation*" (in California this process is called "*conservation*") or ultimately "*liquidation*" should be pursued. Rehabilitation (and, in California, conservation) proceedings seek to restore a financially sick insurer to health, although as we will see in that chapter, these state court proceedings differ from Chapter 11 reorganizations in federal bankruptcy courts which non-insurers can utilize. In a liquidation proceeding, also invariably in state court, an insurance commissioner whom the court has appointed to be liquidator marshals all of the insurer's assets, including any reinsurance recoveries owed to it, and over many years pays claimants according to a set of priority rules set forth in state insurer liquidations laws, such as, for example, Section 7434 of the New York Insurance Law.

V.   ALL INSURANCE COMPANIES MUST COMPLY WITH THE "LAW OF LARGE NUMBERS"

All insurers observe an unwritten law called "the law of large numbers". This "law" holds that the pool of insureds for each insurer must be sufficiently big to reduce the impact of any one loss on the entire pool of insureds. Insurance companies use expert actuaries to quantify specified risks based on models drawn from claims data in prior years. Actuaries measure and predict the "*frequency*" of losses—how often losses do, and will, occur—and their "*severity*"—how big are, and will be, those losses. Very sophisticated and complicated computer models used by actuaries for large U.S. property insurers, for example, attempt to model how often hurricane losses in Florida will happen and how big the resulting property damage claims will be.

Insurers need to attract a risk pool big enough to allow them to withstand projected losses—but not so big that losses are excessive, leaving the insurer financially unable to pay valid claims and allocated and unallocated loss adjustment expenses. Insurers need to collect enough premiums (but not excessive amounts) and earn enough investment income (but not with too risky investments) to pay losses, allocated loss adjustment expenses (e.g. legal fees), unallocated expenses (e.g. rent, IT systems, salaries, etc.) *and* make a reasonable profit. The goal of sound insurance regulation in the U.S. is to foster a system of supervisory policies, procedures, and protocols, in accord with governing laws, which will allow insurance companies to satisfy this fiscal objective and, at the same time, safeguard the rights of policyholders and claimants.

2. The respective roles of state and federal governments in U.S. insurance regulation

Between the founding of the United States in 1776 and the advent of fortress America in 1944 the federal government played virtually no role in regulating insurance, which was considered strictly a local business transaction having no interstate implications. Although unsuccessful attempts were made as early as 1902 for Congress to federalize the regulation of insurers, the only time up until 1944 that the U.S. Government was actively involved in any kind of insurance regulation was the period 1917–1923. That was when (i) Congress enacted the War Risk Insurance Act of 1917 to create the Bureau of War Risk Insurance in the U.S. Treasury Department to offer life insurance to servicemen as well as coverage of merchant marine ships and (ii) the Treasury Department seized the assets of German owned life insurance companies then located in the U.S. and operated those companies in a sort of receivership, thereby making President Woodrow Wilson essentially national insurance commissioner overseeing those German-owned insurers.

I.   BEFORE 1944 INSURANCE WAS DEEMED OUTSIDE THE STREAM OF INTERSTATE COMMERCE

For decades what little regulation of insurance in the U.S. there was, was performed exclusively by state governments. In the early years of the nation state legislatures voted to grant special charters to insurance companies. Beginning in the 1820s, Massachusetts and New York required insurance companies to file financial statements with the State Treasurer and State Comptroller respectively. New Hampshire established the first state insurance department in 1851—actually a board of insurance commissioners, and Massachusetts, Vermont and Rhode Island fol-

lowed soon afterward. New York appointed the first Superintendent of
Insurance in 1859.[1]

In 1869 the U.S. Supreme Court held that an insurance policy was
not an article within the stream of interstate commerce, but was, instead,
a contract made and performed wholly within one state even though the
insurance company might be based in a different state, *Paul v. Virginia*,
75 U.S. 168 (1869). The Court in *Paul* rejected a constitutional claim
under the Commerce Clause (Art. I, Sec. 8, of the U.S. Constitution) by
a Virginia insurance agent convicted of selling a policy without the requisite state license. The agent argued that only Congress could regulate
insurance and that the Virginia licensing law was unconstitutional. For
decades the Supreme Court repeatedly adhered to that position in case
after case.[2]

II.   THE *SOUTH-EASTERN UNDERWRITERS* DECISION WHICH OVERRULED *PAUL*

By 1944, however, property insurance was a multi-billion-dollar business throughout the nation. An investigation by the U.S. Department of
Justice revealed that insurers and producers allegedly conspired in some
states in the South to divide up markets, coerce other agents, brokers and
policyholders to participate in a conspiracy to restrain trade, and boycott
producers who did not cooperate with the asserted conspirators. After an
indictment by the Justice Department under the Sherman Anti-trust Act
was dismissed in the District Court and the dismissal was affirmed on
appeal, the U.S. Supreme Court in *U.S. v. South-Eastern Underwriters
et al*, 322 U.S. 533 (1944) overruled *Paul* and held that insurance was
indeed part of interstate commerce. In a four to three decision, with two
Justices recused, Justice Hugo Black wrote the majority opinion that the
federal government could invoke the civil and criminal provisions of the
federal anti-trust laws to prohibit and sanction anti-competitive conduct
by insurance companies and producers.

---

[1]   S.L. Kimball, "The Purpose of Insurance Regulation: A Preliminary
Inquiry in the Theory of Insurance Law" (1961) 45 *Minn. L. Rev.* 471.
[2]   *See, e.g., New York Life Ins. Co. v. Deer Lodge County*, 231 U.S. 495
(1913).

Justice Black, a former Senator from Alabama, in writing for the four Justices first noted how large and important the property insurance business had become:

> The modern insurance business holds a commanding position in the trade and commerce of our Nation. Built upon the sale of contracts of indemnity, it has become one of the largest and most important branches of commerce. Its total assets exceed $37,000,000,000, or the approximate equivalent of the value of all farm lands and buildings in the United States. Its annual premium receipts exceed $6,000,000,000, more than the average annual revenue receipts of the United States Government during the last decade. Included in the labor force of insurance are 524,000 experienced workers, almost as many as seek their livings in coal mining or automobile manufacturing. Perhaps no modern commercial enterprise directly affects so many persons in all walks of life as does the insurance business. Insurance touches the home, the family, and the occupation or the business of almost every person in the United States.[3]

Then Justice Black distinguished *Paul* and all the cases invoking it by stating that all of those cases involved state laws, not an Act of Congress such as the Sherman Antitrust Act:

> To uphold insurance laws of other states, including tax laws, *Paul v. Virginia's* generalization and reasoning have been consistently adhered to.
>
> Today, however, we are asked to apply this reasoning not to uphold another state law, but to strike down an Act of Congress which was intended to regulate certain aspects of the methods by which interstate insurance companies do business, and, in so doing, to narrow the scope of the federal power to regulate the activities of a great business carried on back and forth across state lines. But past decisions of this Court emphasize that legal formulae devised to uphold state power cannot uncritically be accepted as trustworthy guides to determine Congressional power under the Commerce Clause.[4]

Rejecting various arguments that Congress did not intend to cover insurance companies and producers in the federal anti-trust laws—which contain no specific exception for insurance—Justice Black concluded: "Whether competition is a good thing for the insurance business is not for us to consider. Having power to enact the Sherman Act, Congress did so; if exceptions are to be written into the Act, they must come from the Congress, not this Court."[5]

---

[3]   322 U.S. at 540–41 (footnotes omitted).
[4]   322 U.S. at 545.
[5]   322 U.S. at 561.

Chief Justice Harlan Fiske Stone wrote the main dissent, which Justice Felix Frankfurter joined:

> The power of Congress to regulate interstate communication and transportation incidental to the insurance business is not any more or any less because the number of insurance transactions is great or small. The Congressional power to regulate does not extend to the formation and performance of insurance contracts, save only as the latter may affect communication and transportation which are interstate commerce or may otherwise be found by Congress to affect transactions of interstate commerce. And even then, such effects on the commerce as do not involve restraints in competition in the marketing of goods and services are not within the reach of the Sherman Act. That such are the controlling principles has been fully recognized by this Court in the numerous cases which have held that the business of insurance is not commerce or, as such, subject to the commerce power.[6]

Also dissenting, Justice Robert Jackson discussed the practical implications of the Court suddenly overruling a long line of cases holding states to be the exclusive regulators of insurance:

> Of course, in cases where a constitutional provision or a congressional statute is clear and mandatory, its wisdom is not for us. But the Court now is not following, it is overruling, an unequivocal line of authority reaching over many years. We are not sustaining an act of Congress against attack on its constitutionality, we are making unprecedented use of the Act to strike down the constitutional basis of state regulation. I think we not only are free, but are duty bound, to consider practical consequences of such a revision of constitutional theory... The Court's decision at very least will require an extensive overhauling of state legislation relating to taxation and supervision. The whole legal basis will have to be reconsidered. What will be irretrievably lost and what may be salvaged no one now can say, and it will take a generation of litigation to determine. Certainly, the states lose very important controls and very considerable revenues.[7]

Immediately after the *South-Eastern Underwriters* decision, state insurance officials, insurance company trade associations and insurance producer groups lobbied Congress to legislatively overrule the Supreme Court and restore the states as the sole regulators of the insurance business, including the exclusive power to tax insurance companies. Congress responded by enacting the McCarran-Ferguson Act, 15 U.S.C.

---

[6]   322 U.S. at 568.
[7]   322 U.S. at 589–90.

§§1011 et seq, ("the Act") but did not afford states completely exclusive jurisdiction.

III.   THE BASIC FRAMEWORK OF STATE AND FEDERAL INSURANCE REGULATION CODIFIED IN THE ACT

Under the Act the states may regulate and tax "the business of insurance" unless Congressional legislation enacted into law "specifically relates to the business of insurance" and conflicts with the state law so that the federal statute preempts the state law. The key provision of the Act is Section 2(b) which states:

> No Act of Congress shall be construed to invalidate, impair, or supersede any law enacted by any *State* for the purpose of regulating the business of insurance, or which imposes a fee or tax upon such business, unless such Act specifically relates to the business of insurance: Provided, That after June 30, 1948, the Act of July 2, 1890, as amended, known as *the Sherman Act*, and the Act of October 15, 1914, as amended, known as the *Clayton Act*, and the Act of September 26, 1914, known as the *Federal Trade Commission Act*, as amended [15 U.S.C. 41 et seq.], shall be applicable to the business of insurance to the extent that such business is not regulated by State Law.[8]

The Act also provided that *boycotts, intimidation and coercion were not permissible under any circumstances and* could be enjoined or sanctioned under the Sherman Act, even if a state had allowed such conduct.[9]

In 2021 the Act was amended to provide that it would not apply to "any of the antitrust laws with respect to the business of health insurance (including the business of dental insurance and limited-scope dental benefits)." 15 U.S.C. §1013 added by P.L. 116-327. In the amendatory legislation Congress made clear that it did not intend a wholesale repeal of the Act, and that it would still apply to life and property/casualty insurance, including liability insurance policies, such as, for example, personal automobile insurance policies which provided medical benefits to persons injured in automobile accidents. Also, fearful of upending the health insurance market completely, after over 75 years of virtually complete federal exemption, Congress provided that health insurers were still allowed to act together to (i) collect and disseminate "historical

---

[8]   15 U.S.C. §1012(b).
[9]   15 U.S.C. §§1013–1014.

loss data"—i.e. data on past claims; (ii) determine a "loss development factor—a calculation for adjusting claim reserves to match as nearly as possible what paid losses will be; (iii) perform actuarial services as long as no restraint of trade develops, and (iv) use a standard policy form.[10]

IV.   HOW COURTS HAVE INTERPRETED THE ACT

In various contexts since 1945 the Supreme Court and other federal courts have interpreted and implemented the Act in a variety of contexts. Their decisions have determined whether a federal law, such as, for example, the Employee Retirement Income Security Act of 1974 pre-empts state insurance regulation, or, conversely, whether a state law, such as, for example, Ohio's law according policyholders priority in an insurer liquidation proceeding over unsecured claims of the federal government, should be "reverse preempted" under the Act and given effect, even though a federal statute dictates the opposite result.

In these cases, courts have considered (i) whether the state law regulated "the business of insurance", (ii) whether the federal law *specifically related* to the "business of insurance", (iii) whether the federal law impaired, invalidated or superseded the state law, and (iv) whether the application of federal law would frustrate an express state policy or interfere with a state administrative or judicial proceeding involving insurance. As Justice Ruth Bader Ginsburg wrote in ruling that the federal Racketeer Influenced Corrupt Organizations (RICO) law was applicable to the alleged illegality of certain activities of a health insurer operating in Nevada, even though the state had a law prohibiting unfair claims practices by insurance companies: "When federal law does not directly conflict with state regulation, and when application of the federal law would not frustrate any declared state policy or interfere with a State's administrative regime, the McCarran Ferguson Act does not preclude its application."[11]

Let us examine various examples, which are not intended to be exhaustive, from different fields of law to see how courts have construed the Act:

---

[10]   15 U.S. C. §1013.
[11]   *Humana Inc. v. Forsyth*, 525 U.S. 299, 310 (1999)

1.   Antitrust Law

In several important decisions the Supreme Court interpreted the term "business of insurance" for purposes of determining whether the Act shielded certain arrangements involving insurance companies from federal antitrust scrutiny.[12] In these cases, the Court emphasized that the phrase "business of insurance", for purposes of the antitrust exemption in Section 2(b) of the Act, is not the same as "the business of insurance companies".[13] [14]

The Court established three criteria for deciding whether a challenged practice or arrangement of an insurer constituted the "business of insurance" and therefore would not be subject to federal antitrust strictures: first, whether the practice has the effect of transferring or spreading a policyholder's risk; second, whether the practice is an integral part of the policy relationship between the insurer and the insured; and third, whether the practice is limited to entities within the insurance industry. *See, Royal Drug*, 440 U.S. at 211–12; *Pireno*, 458 U.S. at 129. Applying these three criteria, the Court concluded in *Royal Drug* that a health insurer's agreements with certain pharmacies, to fix charges for prescription drugs and to set the amounts the insurer would pay the pharmacy, were not shielded by the Act from an antitrust suit filed by certain competing pharmacies who alleged that they suffered boycotts when they refused to sign those agreements. Similarly, in *Pireno*, an insurance company's use of a council of chiropractors to assist it in evaluating coverage claims submitted by the plaintiff chiropractor was not outside the scope of the federal antitrust laws where the insurer denied the claims after consulting the committee.

In another aspect of how the Act has been applied to antitrust claims, the Supreme Court and the federal appellate courts have ruled that so long as states exercise even *minimal oversight* as to the rates charged by insurance companies, the Act's exemption from federal antitrust laws will operate. The level of regulation need not be rigorous.[15]

---

[12]   *Group Life & Health Insurance v. Royal Drug Co.*, 440 U.S. 205 (1979) and *Union Labor Life Ins. Co. v. Pireno*, 458 U.S. 119 (1982).

[13]   *Royal Drug*, 440 U.S. at 217.

[14]   *Pireno*, 458 U.S. at 132.

[15]   *See, e.g., FTC v. National Casualty Co.*, 357 U.S. 560 (1958), *Crawford v. Am. Title Ins. Co.*, 518 F.2d 217 (5th Cir. 1975), *Commander Leasing Co. v. Transamerica Title Ins. Co.*, 477 F.2d 77 (10th Cir. 1973) (federal antitrust laws

2.   Arbitration

Federal courts have ruled that a state law nullifying an arbitration clause
in an insurance policy is not "reverse preempted" by the Act, and at least
one federal Circuit Court of Appeals has decided that the Convention on
the Recognition and Enforcement of Foreign Arbitral Awards (known
colloquially as the New York Convention) is a self-executing treaty,
not an "Act of Congress" to which the Act would apply. Therefore,
the Ninth Circuit held that an arbitration clause in a surplus line policy
issued to a business in Washington State could be enforced, even though
Washington State prohibited enforcement of arbitration clauses in insurance policies.[16]

The U.S. Court of Appeals for the Second Circuit took a contrary view
in 1995, holding that the New York Convention was indeed an "Act of
Congress" making the Act applicable and precluding enforcement of an
arbitration clause in an insurance policy.[17] Eventually, the U.S. Supreme
Court could decide to resolve the split among the Circuit Courts of
Appeal, but the weight of authority currently is on the side of enforcing
arbitration clauses in insurance and reinsurance policies, even if a state
law regulating insurance prohibits enforcement.

3.   Banking

In *Barnett Bank of Marion County, N.A. v. Nelson*,[18] the Supreme Court
held that a provision of the federal National Bank Act, 12 U. S. C. § 92,
specifically allowing national banks to sell insurance in certain areas
preempted contrary state insurance laws which prohibited such sales. The

---

reverse preempted because states sufficiently regulated the conduct alleged to be
anti-competitive); *Lawyers Title Co. v. St. Paul Title Ins. Corp.*, 526 F.2d 795
(8th Cir. 1975) (inquiry not a test of state's "zeal and efficiency").

[16]   *See, e.g., CLMS Management Services Limited Partnership v. Amwins
Brokerage of Georgia*, No. 20-35428 (9th Cir. 2021); see also *ESAB Group, Inc.
v. Zurich Ins. PLC*, 685 F.3d 376, 387 (4th Cir. 2012); Safety Nat'l Cas. Corp.
v. Certain Underwriters at Lloyd's, London, 587 F.3d 714 (5th Cir. 2009) (en
banc) (state law prohibiting enforcement of an arbitration clause in an insurance
policy held to be outside the scope of the Act, but not deciding if the New York
Convention is entirely self-executing).

[17]   *Stephens v. American International Insurance Co.*, 66 F.3d 41 (2d Cir.
1995).

[18]   517 U.S. 25 (1996).

Court easily found that the provision legislated by Congress specifically related to the "business of insurance" and therefore invalidated any state laws to the contrary.

4.   Bankruptcy and Insolvency Law

The Supreme Court decided in *United States Dep't of Treasury v. Fabe*,[19] that the federal "super-priority" statute, 31 U. S. C. § 3713(a)(1)(A)(iii), giving claims of the U.S. first priority in any insolvency proceeding was inapplicable, *in part*, to the liquidation of an Ohio insurance company. In the Court's view where state law gave first priority to claims of policyholders and claimants the state law regulated the "business of insurance" by regulating the relationship between and among policyholders, claimants and insurers. Because the federal "super-priority" statute did not specifically relate to the "business of insurance", it thus was "reverse preempted" under the Act.

5.   Civil Rights Law

Two U.S. Circuit Courts of Appeal, a U.S. District Court, and the Texas Supreme Court have construed the Act in cases seeking to invoke the federal Fair Housing Act, 42 U.S.C. §§3601 *et seq*, which prohibits discrimination against members of protected classes of persons in the provision of services relating to housing. The Seventh Circuit ruled in *NAACP v. American Family Mut. Ins. Co.*[20] that the federal Fair Housing Act could be applied to challenge alleged intentional "redlining" by insurer to deny coverage or impose discriminatory rates for homeowners' insurance in certain areas, where no state law specifically permitted the challenged underwriting practices.

By contrast, where an insurers' use of a consumer's credit score was alleged to have an illegal "disparate impact", even if the insurer did not intentionally discriminate, the Ninth Circuit ruled that the Act required an examination of Texas insurance regulations to determine if the insurer had complied with Texas law in using the credit score to raise homeowners' insurance premiums. *Ojo v. Farmers Group*,[21] (en banc) certifying

---

[19]   508 U.S. 491 (1993).
[20]   978 F.2d 287 (7th Cir. 1992).
[21]   600 F.3d 1201 (9th Cir. 2010).

questions to the Texas Supreme Court. The Texas Supreme Court ruled that the plaintiff could not sustain a "disparate impact" claim after the insurer raised his premium for homeowners' insurance based on his credit scores, where Texas insurance regulations expressly allowed insurers to use those scores as a valid underwriting and rating factor, provided they did not intentionally discriminate.[22]

In 2013 the Obama Administration promulgated a regulation from the Department of Housing and Urban Development (HUD) under the Fair Housing Act requiring insurers to justify underwriting and rating practices which allegedly caused an illegal "disparate impact" on protected classes of persons buying homeowners' insurance. The regulation did not provide a blanket defense to the insurer even if the challenged practices complied with applicable state insurance laws. Instead, the regulation allowed insurers to argue that they followed those state regulations, but that argument would be one of several factors for a court in a civil suit, or HUD itself in an administrative proceeding, to consider in determining if the insurer had violated the federal Fair Housing Act.[23]

In 2014 the Property Casualty Insurance Association of America sued the HUD Secretary contending that the regulation violated the Act in not providing insurers a "safe harbor" if they merely showed that their challenged practices complied with state insurance regulations. The federal District Court ruled, in part, for the Association, holding that HUD's failure to adequately assess comments from the Association and from various individual insurers and other insurer groups concerning the application of the Act was arbitrary and capricious, and therefore enjoined enforcement of the regulation pending re-promulgation of the regulation following such an assessment.[24]

In 2016 HUD stated it had assessed the comments from insurers and the Association but decided not to change the regulation. Not surprisingly the Trump Administration issued its own rule in 2020 which did provide for insurers to use the Act as a blanket shield against allegations that they were violating the federal Fair Housing Act. That regulation was stayed by a court injunction, for reasons not specifically related to the Act.

---

[22]   356 S.W.3d 421 (Tx. Sup. Ct. 2011).

[23]   24 C.F.R. pt. 100

[24]   The text of the District Court's decision can be accessed at: 2023https://propertycasualtyfocus.com/wp-content/uploads/2015/08/pciaa-v-donovan.pdf accessed July 10, 2023.

Most recently, in 2021 the Biden Administration started the process of reviving the 2013 Obama Administration fair housing regulation by proposing a rule which again would allow insurers to invoke the Act in defending against allegations they had violated a complainant's civil rights but did not provide insurers with a dispositive "safe harbor". In March 2023 the Biden Administration announced that the regulation would become final.[25] As of March 2023, no homeowners' insurance company has been cited by HUD for allegedly violating the federal Fair Housing Act.[26]

6.   ERISA (Employee Retirement Income Security Act of 1974)

In 1974 the landmark Employee Retirement Income Security Act (ERISA) became federal law which regulates the operation of employer, union, and joint employer-union pension and health plans for retired workers. ERISA contains a specific broad preemption clause for any state law that related to ERISA plans, with a particular exception—considering the McCarran-Ferguson Act—for state laws regulating insurance. However, the legislation also prohibits states from deeming an ERISA plan itself to be an insurance company subject to state insurance regulation. The pertinent provision states:

(a)   Except as provided in subsection (b) of this section, the provisions of this subchapter and subchapter III shall supersede any and all State laws insofar as they may now or hereafter relate to any employee benefit plan described in section 1003(a) of this title and not exempt under section 1003(b) of this title....

(b)   Except as provided in subparagraph (B), nothing in this subchapter shall be construed to exempt or relieve any person from any law of any State which regulates insurance, banking, or securities.

(B)   Neither an employee benefit plan described in section 1003(a) of this title, which is not exempt under section 1003(b) of this title (other than a plan established primarily for the purpose of providing death benefits), nor any trust established under such a plan, shall be deemed to be an insurance company or other insurer, bank, trust company, or investment company or to be engaged in the business of insurance or banking

---

[25]   https://www.hud.gov/sites/dfiles/FHEO/documents/6251-F-02_Discriminatory_Effects_Final_Rule_3-17-23.pdf.

[26]   https://www.regulations.gov/document/HUD-2021-0033-0001   accessed July 10, 2023.

for purposes of any law of any State purporting to regulate insurance companies, insurance contracts, banks, trust companies, or investment companies.[27]

The Supreme Court has issued several decisions interpreting the ERISA preemption clause and the exception for state laws "regulating insurance". In *Metropolitan Life Insurance Co. v. Massachusetts*,[28] the Court sustained a state law that mandated certain mental health benefits to be provided by insurers without regard to whether the covered persons were participants in an ERISA health plan. The Court deemed such a law to be one "which regulates insurance" and therefore not preempted. Similarly, in *Kentucky Assn. of Health Plans, Inc. v. Miller*,[29] the Court ruled that a state law requiring health maintenance organizations and other health insurers to admit "any willing provider" to their networks of participating providers—as long as the provider is licensed and willing to agree to the insurer's terms for network participation—was a law which regulated insurance and therefore not preempted under Section 1144. *See also American Progressive Life Insurance Co. v. Corcoran*,[30] which held that a New York Insurance Department regulation establishing the maximum level of commissions an insurer may pay to agents selling health insurance policies to ERISA health plans was a law which regulates insurance and thus not preempted under Section 1144, even though it affected ERISA health plans.

On the other hand, the Supreme Court ruled in *Pilot Life Insurance Co. v. Dedeaux*,[31] that a Mississippi common law remedy, including the common law cause of action to remedy "bad faith" committed by an insurance company in claims handling—which an ERISA plan participant had invoked to sue the insurer for terminating his coverage—was not saved from preemption under Section 1144. The Court ruled that the state common law cause of action were not specifically directed at an insurance company but could be invoked for any breach of contract action in Mississippi. In respect of the McCarran-Ferguson Act, of the factors for

---

[27]   29 U.S.C. § 1144.
[28]   471 U.S. 724 (1985).
[29]   538 U.S. 329 (2003).
[30]   715 F.2d 784 (2d Cir. 1983).
[31]   481 U.S. 41 (1987).

determining if a state law regulated the "business of insurance", the state common law causes of action for the insurer's alleged bad faith:

> does not define the terms of the relationship between the insurer and the insured; it declares only that, whatever terms have been agreed upon in the insurance contract, a breach of that contract may in certain circumstances allow the policyholder to obtain punitive damages. The state common law of bad faith is therefore no more "integral" to the insurer-insured relationship than any State's general contract law is integral to a contract made in that State.[32]

Therefore, the McCarran-Ferguson Act did not support the insured's argument that the state law was not preempted under Section 1144.

7.   RICO (Racketeer Influenced Corrupt Organizations Act)

State unfair claims practice laws complement but do not conflict with the federal RICO Act, and therefor do not reverse preempt the federal statute. So the Supreme Court decided in *Humana Inc. v. Forsyth*, 525 U.S. 299 (1999). A health insurer defending a RICO suit was unsuccessful in arguing that RICO was inapplicable because it was already subject to Nevada unfair claims practices laws which prohibited the same type of alleged fraud addressed by the federal RICO statute:

> [W]e see no frustration of state policy in the RICO litigation at issue here. RICO's private right of action and treble damages provision appears to complement Nevada's statutory and common-law claims for relief. In this regard, we note that Nevada filed no brief at any stage of this lawsuit urging that application of RICO to the alleged conduct would frustrate any state policy or interfere with the State's administrative regime.[33]

8.   Securities Law

The Supreme Court sided with the federal Securities & Exchange Commission and held that sales of variable annuities were "securities" within the Commission's jurisdiction, even though those same products could also be regulated by states under their respective insurance laws.[34]

---

[32]   481 U.S. at 51.

[33]   525 U.S. at 313.

[34]   *SEC v. Variable Annuity Life Ins. Co.*, 359 U.S. 65 (1959) (federal securities laws applied to variable annuities even though they had features resembling insurance where issuer did not assume risk of fluctuation in value of investments).

In another ruling upholding federal jurisdiction, the Supreme Court decided that securities fraud claims could be brought against the company under federal securities laws even though claims concerned statements made by a defendant as to a proposed merger of insurance companies, and the merger was approved by a state insurance commissioner.[35]

9.   Federal Legislation Affecting State Insurance Regulation

Product Liability Risk Retention Act of 1981, Pub. L .No. 97-45, and Liability Risk Retention Act of 1986, Pub. L. No. 99-563

In these two enactments Congress expressly preempted state insurance rules which prohibited or severely restricted groups of product manufacturers and then service providers, such as doctors, psychologists, lawyers, architects, and others engaged in the same business or profession, from joining together to form their own insurance entity to provide commercial liability insurance for each member. These are not ordinary commercial insurance companies, but, rather, "risk retention groups" (RRGs) owned by the member insureds and professionally managed by large brokers and professional risk managers. In Chapter 4 we examine RRGs in detail as a federally mandated exception to state insurer licensing rules.

In the 1986 legislation Congress also preempted state insurance laws which had prevented persons engaged in the same business or profession from purchasing group commercial liability insurance. Insurance purchased on a group basis is usually cheaper because the insurance company does not have to incur the costs of underwriting and rating each individual risk. The 1986 law expressly contemplates that members of a registered purchasing group will benefit from lower rates, although states may still require the insurance company to comply with state policy form and rating laws.[36]

These two federal laws only deal with *commercial liability insurance.* States remain free to prohibit or restrict group property insurance and group personal lines insurance such as personal automobile insurance for private passenger vehicles.[37]

---

[35]   *SEC v. National Securities, Inc.,* 393 U.S. 453 (1969).
[36]   *Insurance Company of Pennsylvania v. Corcoran,* 850 F.2d 88 (2d. Cir. 1988).
[37]   *See, e.g.,* N.Y. Ins. Dept. Opinion of the General Counsel, OGC Op. No. 06-04-08, accessible at: https://www.dfs.ny.gov/insurance/ogco2006/rg060408 .htm accessed July 10, 2023.

10.   Bank Sales of Insurance Allowed by Congress

In 1999 and again in 2010 Congress enacted legislation which dramatically affected and, to some extent expressly preempted, state insurance regulation. First, the Gramm-Leach-Bliley Act, Pub. L. No. 106-102 (1999) explicitly allowed any "depositary institution", i.e. a bank, or an affiliate of a bank, to sell insurance, if licensed by a state, notwithstanding that the state may have long prohibited banks from selling insurance.[38] In preempting such state prohibitions, Congress expressly referred to the Supreme Court's decision in *Barnett Bank of Marion County, N.A. v. Nelson*,[39] discussed at page 16–17 above, interpreting the McCarran-Ferguson Act. Nevertheless, Congress specifically allowed states to continue to enforce laws designed to promote consumer protection in the sale of insurance, by banks and any other persons or entities licensed as agents, such as prohibitions on misleading advertising of insurance, and prohibiting a bank from "tying" the sale of insurance to another product or service like conditioning the issuance of a mortgage on the purchase of insurance from that bank.[40]

An excellent, detailed analysis of federal laws affecting bank sales of insurance and preemption of state insurance rules prior to, and after, the passage of the Gramm-Leach-Bliley Act can be found in a 2001 article for the North Carolina Banking Institute published by the University of North Carolina School of Law.[41]

11.   The Federal Insurance Office

Another federal law which significantly altered the relationship between the federal government and state laws regulating insurance is the Dodd-Frank Wall Street Reform and Consumer Protection Act of 2010, Pub. L. No. 111-203 (2010). Besides legislating major changes in how large financial institutions involved in the 2008–09 financial crisis would henceforth be supervised, in Title V of this law Congress created the

---

[38]   15 U.S.C. §6701(d)(2)(A).
[39]   517 U.S. 25 (1996).
[40]   15 U.S.C. § 6701(d)(2)(B).
[41]   Scott A. Sinder, "Gramm-Leach-Bliley Act and State Regulation of the Business of Insurance-Past, Present and … Future", 5 *N.C. Banking Inst.* 49 (2001), accessible at: http://scholarship.law.unc.edu/ncbi/vol5/iss1/5 accessed July 10, 2023.

first federal agency devoted exclusively to analyzing how insurance was regulated in the U.S.—the Federal Insurance Office (FIO) located within the Department of the Treasury. The Director of the FIO is not a Presidential appointee; rather, she or he is appointed by the Secretary of the Treasury.[42]

The FIO does not have the power to directly regulate insurers, except in one limited instance discussed below, but mainly acts as a repository of information about insurers and insurance regulation which Congress and the Executive can access. However, the FIO does have subpoena power to obtain information from most insurers and their affiliates, although it is required to first access publicly available data, and the FIO has no jurisdiction at all over health insurance, most long-term care insurance policies, and crop insurance.[43]

The one instance in which the FIO can directly change state insurance rules stems from its power to conclude international trade agreements in conjunction with the U.S. Office of Trade Representative, and to preempt any state insurance law which "(A) results in less favorable treatment of a non-United States insurer domiciled in a foreign jurisdiction that is subject to a covered agreement than a United States insurer domiciled, licensed, or otherwise admitted in that State; and (B) is inconsistent with a covered agreement." To prevent the FIO from riding roughshod over state insurance rules, Congress prescribed a lengthy consultative process with any state whose law might be preempted, which the FIO must utilize before it can exercise the power to preempt a particular state insurance law that it determines is inconsistent with a "covered agreement".[44]

The FIO did negotiate two such "covered agreements" in recent years, one with the U.K. and one with the EU, addressing how reinsurers domiciled in the U.K. and EU, which were unlicensed in a U.S. state, would be governed by state insurance rules. As we will see in Chapter 5, those rules directly applied to licensed insurers who bought reinsurance from unlicensed, non-U.S. reinsurers: if the licensed direct insurer wanted to take credit on its filed financial statements for the reinsurance—which virtually every licensed insurance company does—it first must obtain contractual commitments from the unlicensed non-U.S. reinsurer to establish a trust for the exclusive benefit of the licensed direct insurer,

---

[42]   31 U.S.C. § 313(b).
[43]   31 U.S.C. §§ 313(d), (f), (k).
[44]   31 U.S.C. §§ 313(f), 314.

or purchase a letter of credit from a qualified bank or trust company, to cover all of the liabilities which the unlicensed reinsurer would owe to the licensed direct insurer. The two "covered agreements" negotiated by the FIO respectively enabled reinsurers domiciled in the U.K. and EU countries to avoid those onerous and expensive security arrangements whenever they sold reinsurance to licensed direct insurers. By September 2022, after a five-year transition period, every state was required to stop enforcing any laws that were inconsistent with the two covered agreements, and every state complied.

12.   The Financial Stability Oversight Council

The Dodd-Frank Act also provided for the creation of the Financial Stability Oversight Council (FSOC) within the U.S. Treasury Dept. The Treasury Secretary chairs the FSOC, and its other members are the heads of federal financial regulatory agencies, e.g. Securities and Exchange Commission and Commodities Future Trading Commission, along with one member with insurance expertise appointed by the President. The Director of the FIO is a non-voting member of the FSOC.[45]

The main function of the FSOC is to designate major banks and other financial institutions, with more than $50 billion in assets, as "systemically important". These "systemically important financial institutions"— SIFIs—are subject to more stringent supervision by the Federal Reserve, including higher capital and greater liquidity requirements.[46]

The FSOC designated three insurance holding companies: AIG which consented to the designation, Prudential which contested its designation administratively but did not seek judicial review, and MetLife which successfully sued the FSOC in federal court with the U.S. District Court finding that MetLife's designation was arbitrary and capricious.[47]

The government dropped its appeal of the *MetLife* decision to the D.C. Circuit in 2018. In 2017 the FSOC voted to de-designate AIG, and in 2018 the FSOC voted to de-designate Prudential. Since then, no holding company owning an insurer has been designated as "systemically important" and required to be supervised stringently by the Federal Reserve.

---

[45]   12 U.S.C. § 5321.
[46]   12 U.S.C. § 5323.
[47]   *MetLife, Inc. v. Financial Stability Oversight Council*, 177 F.Supp.3d 219 (D.D.C. 2016).

3. How state insurance departments are organized and operate

I. THE ORGANIZATION OF STATE INSURANCE DEPARTMENTS

Insurance departments are agencies of state governments, but in many U.S. states, they are not financed from general taxes. Instead, state insurance departments receive fees for issuing licenses and conducting examinations, and/or assessments from insurers in proportion to how much premium those insurers wrote in that state, in relation to all other life or property/casualty insurers, in the preceding year.

Most states have commissioners appointed by the elected governors to whom they report, but some states, most notably California, North Carolina, and the State of Washington, have elected commissioners who do not report to governors and cannot be removed by governors. Commissioners generally appoint the most important officials of the department, such as the chief deputy commissioner and general counsel.

Except for the top officials most state insurance department employees are career civil servants who must pass competitive examinations to be hired and promoted. Most states have a single agency regulating solely insurance, but a few states such as Vermont, New Jersey and, most recently, New York have agencies regulating both banking and insurance. California has separate agencies regulating insurers and managed care companies; in New York the Department of Financial Services and Department of Health respectively do so.

Some state insurance departments have units that correspond to the kind of insurance they regulate, for example, life, property, and health. Other departments, such as in California and Texas, are organized by function with different bureaus—one for regulating all insurers' financial condition and one for regulating how all insurers deal with consumers.

II.   THE MAIN FUNCTIONS OF STATE INSURANCE DEPARTMENTS

1.   Issuing Licenses to Insurance Companies and Insurance Professionals

As discussed later in Chapter 4, the state licensing process for insurance companies and insurance professionals, such as agents, brokers, producers, and adjusters, involves a set of qualifications and criteria intended to ensure that insurers are financed adequately and managed with competence and integrity. Similarly, licensing of insurance professionals, both residents and non-residents of the state, seeks to give licenses only to persons who are both competent and trustworthy. Although in recent years states have attempted to harmonize their respective licensing processes to effect greater uniformity, there are still significant variations among the states in the process for licensing insurance companies.

Although states do not license excess line or surplus line insurers, they do license the brokers who are permitted to place insurance with them, and state insurance regulators work with associations of those brokers to determine whether a particular unlicensed insurer satisfies the requirements, such as having a requisite trust fund and being licensed by a qualified domicile—for example, Bermuda or the United Kingdom (U.K.)—with a robust system of insurance regulation, so as to be an "approved" surplus line or excess line insurer.

Similarly, although states do not license most foreign or alien reinsurers, they do require licensed ceding companies to comply with rules allowing them to take credit for the reinsurance on their filed financial statements only if the unlicensed reinsurers satisfy certain criteria, such as having a policyholder surplus exceeding $250 million, being domiciled in a qualified jurisdiction, and agreeing to be sued in U.S. courts. Alternatively, if a licensed ceding company wishes to buy reinsurance from an unlicensed company that does not satisfy these standards, state insurance departments insist that the licensed ceding carrier require, by contract, that the unlicensed reinsurer maintain a trust fund, or post a letter of credit from a licensed bank, or employ reinsurance accounting measures sufficient to pay valid claims and allocated loss adjustment expenses and return unearned premiums.

2.   Monitoring the Solvency of Licensed Insurance Companies

The most important function which a state insurance department performs is to make sure that insurance companies which it licenses to transact business in that state have a policyholder surplus sufficient to pay all valid claims. State insurance regulators utilize a variety of tools, and often coordinate with other state insurance departments, to achieve this objective. These are detailed in Chapter 5.

As explicated in Chapter 6, when an insurer encounters financial difficulty, the state insurance department of its domicile determines whether to place the insurer under enhanced regulatory oversight through a process known as "administrative supervision" which is typically confidential. If an insurer is insolvent or in "hazardous financial condition" the domestic state insurance department seeks an order from a specified court in that state placing the insurer into public rehabilitation or liquidation proceedings.

3.   Supervising the Market Conduct of Licensees

Insurance departments oversee how licensed insurers interact with policyholders and claimants in terms of processing claims promptly and fairly, advertising insurance truthfully, addressing consumer complaints responsibly, underwriting and rating their policies without unfair discrimination, canceling and non-renewing policies in accord with applicable state laws, and writing their policies comprehensibly in "plain English". Such regulation is discussed in Chapter 7. States also enforce rules that require agents and brokers to handle policyholder premium funds in a fiduciary capacity and prohibit them from comingling premium funds, which must be forwarded to insurers, with the agent or broker's own commissions or other personal funds.

States routinely enforce their respective market conduct rules through enforcement proceedings involving a written notice of specific charges and a hearing before an administrative hearing officer usually appointed by the department bringing the charges. *See, e.g.,* N.Y. Ins. L. § 2110. Although some have questioned the independence of these hearing officers, the hearing process frequently leads to a formal administrative determination that the respondent has violated one or more provisions of the state's insurance statute or departmental regulations. Often insurance companies and professionals choose to settle with departments and to execute stipulations or consent orders admitting to the violations and agreeing to pay financial penalties, in some cases, totaling millions of dollars. Particularly with individuals, if no settlement occurs, state insurance regulators can and do issue administrative "cease and desist" orders—often in the case of activity by persons lacking a requisite license—and suspensions or even revocations of agent, broker, producer or adjuster licenses.[1]

4.   Issuing Regulations

Departments frequently issue regulations to give details as to how they will implement various insurance statutes passed by the legislatures in their states. These regulations can be very detailed, such as New York's lengthy regulation prescribing all of the various provisions that health insurance policies sold in New York must contain,[2] or relatively simple, *e.g.* the Massachusetts Division of Insurance regulation on coverage for motorcycles.[3]

5.   Initiating Prosecutions

Departments also directly undertake criminal investigations, or assist prosecutors, concerning insurance fraud. For example, the New York State Department of Financial Services has cooperated with the police and prosecutors to arrest a number of doctors, lawyers and other persons involved in staging fake automobile accidents and submitting bogus claims as a means of illegally claiming benefits under auto insurance policies.

6.   Coordinating—to a Greater or Lesser Extent—with the State Attorney General's Offices

In recent years state attorneys general have increasingly investigated, prosecuted, and executed agreements with insurance companies and insurance producers charged with violating various state consumer pro-

---

[1]   *See, e.g.,* https://www.tdi.texas.gov/orders/co020487.html (last visited July 11, 2023).
[2]   11 N.Y.C.R.R. Part 52.
[3]   211 CMR 3.00.

tection laws. Sometimes these proceedings occur entirely independent of state insurance departments.[4]

At other times, these enforcement actions by state attorney general offices run parallel with separate proceedings initiated by state insurance departments alleging the same misconduct as violating one or more insurance laws. The New York Attorney General's investigation of both insurers and producers over the contingent commissions paid to large producers for deceptive conduct in 2004 and 2005 is the most prominent example of a major enforcement proceeding brought by a state attorney general, followed by a separate administrative proceeding initiated by an insurance department.[5]

7.   Responding to Freedom of Information Law or Records Access Law Requests

Based on the federal Freedom of Information Act (FOIA) (5 U.S.C. § 552), most U.S. states now have similar laws allowing anyone to request a copy of a public record from state agencies, including various insurance departments.[6] For the nominal cost of copying documents, a person can access many, though not all, of the records compiled by a state insurance department, including, e.g. filed reports on examination of licensed insurers, records of disciplinary proceedings brought against insurance companies and insurance professionals, and correspondence between a department and an insurer or counsel for the insurer. For access to be granted, it is necessary to specify in as much detail as possible exactly what records are being sought, and it is helpful to specify the approximate month(s) and year(s) the records were generated by the department and/ or submitted to the department.

---

[4]   *See, e.g.,* https://legalnewsline.com/stories/511433212-mass-attorney -general-secures-244-000-from-delaware-life-insurance-after-concerns-over -annuity-payments and https://www.mass.gov/doc/health-e-systems-aod (last visited July 11, 2023).

[5]   *See, e.g.,* Stipulation of Settlement with the ACE Limited et al, https:// www.sec.gov/Archives/edgar/data/896159/000119312506092893/dex102.htm (last visited July 11, 2023).

[6]   *See, e.g.,* Louisiana R.S. § 44:1 *et seq.*; N.Y. Pub. Off. L. § 84 *et seq.*; Ore. R.S. § 192.311 *et seq.*

Some states, such as New York, have a webpage on their insurance department website for submitting a FOIA request.[7] The Texas Attorney General's Office has published a Handbook for submitting FOIA requests to Texas state agencies, including the Texas Department of Insurance.[8] The National Freedom of Information Coalition, a private, nonprofit organization, maintains a useful website with links to various state FOIA laws, sample FOIA requests to use in requesting records, and a newsletter highlighting developments in litigation involving state FOIA laws.[9] Note that almost every state FOIA law exempts trade secrets and clearly proprietary information submitted to an insurance department by insurance companies.[10] Some insurance regulatory laws, such as, e.g. state insurer holding company acts discussed in Chapter 5 as a key solvency regulatory tool, explicitly exempt certain documents submitted by an insurer under those laws.[11] Nevertheless, state courts have sometimes been quite resistant to efforts by insurance companies to shield documents they submitted from public access, without a convincing showing that the documents contain proprietary data to such an extent that they are virtually certain to suffer economic harm from competitors if the exemption did not apply. For example, in *Markowiz v. Serio*,[12] the New York Court of Appeals, that state's highest court, ruled that an insurer had not proved that it would likely suffer substantial competitive harm if data it was required to submit—containing information on cancellations and non-renewals of automobile insurance policies broken down by zip code—were disclosed to the public.[13] If a FOIA request for records from a U.S. state insurance department is found by a reviewing court to have been rejected without proper justification, or if the insurance department fails to comply with specified time limits for responding to a FOIA

---

[7] https://www.dfs.ny.gov/contact_us/foil_requests (last visited July 11, 2023).

[8] https://www.texasattorneygeneral.gov/sites/default/files/files/divisions/ open-government/publicinfo_hb.pdf (last visited July 11, 2023).

[9] https://www.nfoic.org (last visited July 11, 2023).

[10] *See, e.g.,* N.Y. Pub. Off. L. § 87(2)(d).

[11] *See, e.g.,* Tex. Ins. Code § 823.011.

[12] 11 N.Y.3d 43 (2008).

[13] *See also*: *Washington Post Co. v. New York State Insurance Dept.*, 61 NY.2d 557 (1984) (ruling that minutes of directors' meetings of insurance companies are not automatically exempt in their entirety as proprietary information, and that insurers would have to clearly establish they were entitled to the exemption for those portions of minutes assertedly containing proprietary information).

request, under many state FOIA law the requesting party can recover reasonable attorney's fees and court costs for prosecuting the litigation.[14]

8.   Defending the Validity of an Insurance Department Regulations and Enforcement Rulings

State insurance departments are sometimes sued in court by insurance companies or insurance professionals aggrieved by certain regulations which they contend are "arbitrary and capricious", or by persons and entities who or which the departments have found in administrative hearings to have violated one or more provisions of state insurance laws. Typically, the state attorney general's office represents the insurance department in such litigation.

State judges have historically been reluctant to "second guess" the actions of a state insurance department's expert staff and have accorded broad discretion to a defendant insurance commissioner to implement the state's insurance regulations as she or he determines best.[15] On the other hand, when an insurance commissioner has clearly ignored the plain wording of a state statute, state courts have not hesitated to invalidate regulations issued by an insurance department for being "ultra vires" or lacking the requisite statutory authority.[16]

Persons or entities who or which have been administratively sanctioned for violating one or more of the state's insurance regulatory laws or who have been denied a license, such as an insurance agent's license, have had even less success in persuading state courts that the insurance

---

[14]   *See, e.g.,* N.Y. Pub. Off. L. § 89.

[15]   *See, e.g., Medical Malpractice Insurance Assn. v. Superintendent of Insurance,* 72 N.Y.2d 753 (N.Y. Ct. App. 1988) (upholding as reasonable Superintendent of Insurance's determination to limit increase in medical malpractice insurance rates and explicitly stating it would not question Superintendent's expertise in doing so) *citing N.Y. Public Interest Research Group v. State Insurance Dept.,* 66 N.Y.2d 444 (N.Y. Ct. of App. 1985).

[16]   *See, e.g., National Association of Mutual Insurance Companies v. Office of Insurance Commissioner of the State of Washington,* No. 22-2-00180-34 (Superior Ct. 2022) (invalidating ban on insurers' use of credit scoring as lacking in statutory authority) accessible at https://www.insurance.wa.gov/sites/default/files/documents/thurston-county-superior-court-final-order.pdf; https://www.insurance.wa.gov/news/final-order-courts-credit-scoring-decision-kreidler-will-not-appeal (last visited July 11, 2023).

department made its rulings without substantial evidence on the whole record.[17]

BOX 3.1   PRACTICAL TIPS FOR PRACTITIONERS

Practitioners instructed to sue U.S. state insurance regulators for acting arbitrarily and capriciously in issuing a regulation which a client finds intolerable, or for taking an enforcement action which may not be based on substantial evidence following a hearing, should be aware that many jurisdictions prescribe exceedingly short limitations periods for such suits. For example, New York has a relatively short four-month limitations period in Section 213 of its Civil Practice Law and Rules running from the date the department's determination becomes effective. Given the accelerated time requirements and the relatively poor chances of success in such litigation, and the likely negative reaction among insurance department staff to being sued which could adversely affect a licensee who sued them unsuccessfully, practitioners should seek ways of resolving an insurance client's problem through negotiation and consensual resolution with department staff. Only where the client is so severely affected by a state insurance department's policy as to be unable to profitably do business in that state and only where the law is arguably unsettled should litigation be utilized, and in that exceedingly rare circumstance, the practitioner and client must (i) retain local qualified counsel who is expert in successfully prosecuting such suits and (ii) attempt to enlist as many insurance industry allies as possible to request permission from the court to file supportive briefs as *amici curiae*.

9.   Supervising Operation of Statutory Residual Markets

For certain mandatory coverages such as motor vehicle insurance which states require vehicle owners to have, or property insurance which,

---

[17]   *See, e.g., Zaal v. Texas Dept. of Insurance*, (Ct. of App. 2013) https://casetext.com/case/zaal-v-tex-dept-of-ins (last visited July 11, 2023), *citing Brown v. Texas Dept. of Insurance*, 34 S.W.3d 683 (Ct. of App. 2000); *David v. Comm. of Insurance*, 53 Mass. App. Ct. 162 (Ct. of App. 2001); *Goldberg v. Barger*, 37 Cal. App. 3d 988 (Ct. of App. 1974).

because of hurricanes and other natural disasters—or because of adverse neighborhood conditions—may be unaffordable or unavailable, U.S. state insurance regulators supervise the operation of "residual markets". If a person cannot obtain an automobile insurance policy or a homeowners' policy from licensed insurers in a state, she or he can buy one from a non-profit organization created to be "the insurer of last resort". State insurance regulators approve the various Plans of Operations for these organizations which typically involve licensed insurers having to take an assigned percentage of eligible risks each year, based on how much relevant insurance the insurer wrote in the state the prior year. The premium rates for such coverage are usually set substantially higher than what commercial insurers are allowed to charge in the so-called "voluntary market". A detailed discussion of each state's residual market plans can be found on the website of AIPSO, an organization which helps administer the various plans.[18]

10.   **Apprising Industry and Counsel about Relevant Statutes, Regulations, Enforcement Actions, and Informal Regulatory Guidance**

The website of each state insurance department usually contains links to the statutory insurance code, the department's regulations, and bulletins or other department announcements implementing the state's insurance regulatory laws.[19] The New York Department of Financial Services has posted all in-force Circular Letters, which are essentially bulletins and represent the Department's then current view of how the New York Insurance Law and Department regulations should be applied, although a Circular Letter itself does not have the force of law unlike a statute or a Department regulation.[20]

Some state regulators have helpfully posted enforcement actions, allowing insurers, producers, other insurance professionals and their

---

[18]   https://www.aipso.com/Portals/0/AIPSOOpenAccess/AIPSO-Value-to -Industry-3-2023.pdf?ver=2023-03-23-093425-930 (last visited July 11, 2023).

[19]   *See, e.g.,* California Department of Insurance website https://www .insurance.ca.gov/0250-insurers/0500-legal-info/ (last visited July 11, 2023); Texas Department of Insurance website https://www.tdi.texas.gov/commissioner/ code.html (last visited July 11, 2023).

[20]   https://www.dfs.ny.gov/industry_guidance/circular_letters (last visited July 11, 2023).

counsel to evaluate how similarly situated respondents were penalized for various regulatory violations.[21]

New York's insurance regulatory agency had issued useful opinions of the Office of General Counsel in the Insurance Department up until the merger of that agency with the Banking Department in 2011 to create the present Department of Financial Services. Unfortunately, no additional opinions have been published since then. Nevertheless, opinions from 2000 to 2011, which, one must note, are informal and subject to modification or withdrawal, can be accessed at: https://www.dfs.ny.gov/industry_guidance/interpretations_and_opinions (last visited July 11, 2023).

11.   Informing Consumers about Various Kinds of Insurance

State insurance departments usually provide helpful information on their websites about (i) which insurers, producers, and other licensees hold active licenses in that state, and (ii) what consumers should know about buying life insurance, health insurance, automobile insurance and homeowner/renter insurance.[22]

III.   HOW STATES COORDINATE THEIR ACTIVITIES THROUGH THE NATIONAL ASSOCIATION OF INSURANCE COMMISSIONERS (NAIC)

In 1871 New York and several other states which had established separate insurance departments formed the National Association of Insurance Commissioners (NAIC) to exchange information about regulatory practices. Today every state, the District of Columbia, Puerto Rico, Virgin Islands, Guam, American Samoa and the Northern Marianas Islands

---

[21]   *See, e.g.,* https://www.dfs.ny.gov/industry_guidance/enforcement_actions_lfs (last visited July 11, 2023).

[22]   *See, e.g.,* Missouri Insurance Department website: https://sbs.naic.org/solar-external-lookup/#_ga=2.194936685.1756245890.1569421886-2135126394.1564941287 (last visited July 11, 2023); https://insurance.mo.gov/consumers/ ; Wyoming Insurance Department website (last visited July 11, 2023): https://www.sircon.com/ComplianceExpress/Inquiry/consumerInquiry.do?nonSscrb=Y (last visited July 11, 2023); https://doi.wyo.gov/consumers (last visited July 11, 2023).

belong to it. The NAIC is headed by officers elected by the vote of all commissioners.

It is critical to understand that, although comprised of governmental officials, the NAIC itself is *not* a government agency, and the model laws and regulations it promulgates for states to consider adopting are not themselves official legislative or administrative acts. Instead, the NAIC is a nonprofit organization whose funds are derived partly from dues paid by the member states and territories, but mainly from fees paid by insurers, producers, and others, like attorneys, who (i) utilize various NAIC electronic portals for required filings, (ii) purchase NAIC publications, e.g. handbooks used by state insurance department examiners, and (iii) attend NAIC national meetings in various cities held three times a year.

The NAIC considers and issues model laws and model regulations on various aspects of insurance supervision, most recently, to take two examples, on data security and corporate governance of insurance companies, strictly in the nature of advisory recommendations to state insurance departments and state legislators, like the model laws promulgated by the American Law Institute. The NAIC also issues detailed accounting rules for insurers to follow in preparing the quarterly and annual financial statements that they must file with state insurance departments. Every state has officially adopted most of these accounting rules, and some state insurance codes expressly refer to them as being applicable to insurers.[23]

In two instances the *activities* of the NAIC, not the model laws or regulations, have been expressly incorporated into federal law, as we shall see in more detail in Chapter 4 and Chapter 5. First, the 2010 Dodd-Frank Act streamlined state regulation of unlicensed surplus line or excess line insurers, and one of the provisions explicitly requires states to allow licensed surplus line or excess line brokers, if all other conditions are met, to place coverage with unlicensed alien insurance companies listed on the Quarterly Listing of Alien Insurers maintained by the NAIC International Insurers Department.[24] In the second instance, the Dodd-Frank Act provided that only the domestic state of the direct, ceding insurer may regulate the reinsurance arrangements of that licensed

---

[23]   *See, e.g.,* Tex. Admin. Code Rule § 7.18 (incorporating NAIC Accounting Manual by reference with stated exceptions).

[24]   15 U.S.C. § 8204(b).

domestic insurer, provided that the domestic state is one which the NAIC has "accredited" or meets the standards for such accreditation.[25]

In the early 1990s the NAIC and state insurance regulators were the subject of intense criticism by influential Congressmen who considered their regulation of weak insurance companies far too lax in the wake of numerous insurer insolvencies that occurred beginning in the mid-1980s. These legislators advocated that specific federal regulatory standards be established for all state insurance departments to meet. Representative John Dingell, the then powerful Chair of the House Energy and Commerce Committee, prepared scathing reports and held probing hearings on the deficiencies of state insurance regulation.[26]

Beginning in 1990, in response to such intense Congressional criticism and fearful that federal regulation of insurance would displace their jurisdiction, the NAIC and its members undertook to improve the quality of state insurance regulation nationwide by establishing an "accreditation" regime. A state insurance department would be accredited only if it had enacted and properly enforced various NAIC Model Laws, such as the Model Insurer Holding Company Systems Act and the NAIC Model Managing General Agents Act, and only if the department had sufficient resources to enforce a robust financial solvency program.

Today every state insurance department, along with the insurance regulatory agencies in the District of Columbia and the U.S. Virgin Islands, is accredited under the NAIC's criteria.[27] By 2010 when the Dodd-Frank Act was passed, the NAIC's reputation specifically, and the standing of state insurance regulators generally, had improved over the intervening period such that in Section 531 of that statute Congress conditioned its reinsurance regulatory streamlining, discussed in Chapter 5, on the NAIC accreditation program. Additionally, a report to Congress in 2013 from the U.S. Government Accountability Office indicated how successfully

---

[25] 15 U.S.C. § 8221.
[26] *See, e.g.* Cohen, "A quest for a national policy to cover insurance industry risk", *Chicago Tribune*, Mar 24, 1991; Testimony of the Asst. Comptroller General before the Subcommittee on Oversight and Investigations, https://www.gao.gov/assets/t-ggd-93-26.pdf (last visited July 11, 2023); U.S. House of Representatives, Committee on Energy and Commerce, Subcommittee on Oversight and Investigations, *Failed Promises: Insurance Company Insolvencies*, 101st Cong., 2nd Sess., Committee Print 101-P (Washington: GPO 1990); The Federal Insurance Solvency Act (H.R. 4900, 1992).
[27] https://content.naic.org/cipr-topics/accreditation (last visited July 11, 2023).

state insurance regulators were able to limit the adverse impact on insurance companies of the 2008–09 financial crisis.[28]

The NAIC maintains an extensive set of public and confidential databases about insurers and others involved in the insurance business.

- One public database contains all the financial statements filed by insurers with one or more insurance departments.
- Another public database shows all the non-U.S. insurers which meet the requirements for approved "surplus line" insurers.
- A third confidential database that is open only to regulators and the Federal Insurance Office contains information about ongoing and prior investigations of insurers, producers and other licensees of state insurance departments.

The NAIC operates two electronic portals:

(i)   one used by state insurance departments to allow consumers and others to see if a particular individual or business entity is licensed by one or more of those states as a producer or in the case of a company, as a licensed insurer;[29] and

(ii)   a service called the National Insurance Producer Registry (NIPR) which agents, brokers and producers use to obtain and renew licenses from various states in which they transact insurance.[30]

BOX 3.2   PRACTICAL TIP FOR PRACTITIONERS:

Often the website of an insurance department will show the specific examiner, with an email address, responsible for the topic of interest. *See, e.g.,* New York State Dept. of Fin. Serv. Insurance Circular Letter No. 12 on Climate Change (2020) at https://www.dfs.ny.gov/industry _guidance/circular_letters/cl2020_15 (last visited July 11, 2023). If no examiner is identified for the topic of interest on the relevant department website, the NAIC webpage of state insurance departments contains a useful directory of each state's insurance department personnel,

---

[28]   https://www.gao.gov/products/gao-13-583 (last visited July 11, 2023).
[29]   https://sbs.naic.org/solar-external-lookup/#_ga=2.194936685.1756245890 .1569421886-2135126394.1564941287 (last visited July 11, 2023).
[30]   https://nipr.com (last visited July 11, 2023).

listed by function, with telephone numbers, although the information may not be completely current.[31]

NAIC model laws and model regulations, as well as the handbooks used by insurance regulators in examining an insurance company's financial condition and market conduct, are available for purchase.[32]

IV. STATE INSURANCE DEPARTMENTS ALSO WORK WITH THE NATIONAL COUNCIL OF INSURANCE LEGISLATORS (NCOIL)

A separate non-governmental organization, comprised only of state legislators involved with insurance, is the National Council of Insurance Legislators (NCOIL), created in 1969. Like the NAIC but having an active membership of fewer than half the states, NCOIL issues model laws on various insurance regulatory topics, and zealously advocates for state insurance regulation with very limited preemption by the federal government.[33]

Most insurance commissioners are appointed by Governors who, of course, are elected independently of the legislator members of NCOIL, and are often from opposing political parties. In states like California and North Carolina the commissioners are themselves elected officials who work with but, of course, do not report to legislators who may be of a different political party in those states. Naturally the views of a particular commissioner in a state, on one or more insurance regulatory issues and the collective positions of the commissioners as expressed through the NAIC, will sometimes differ from those of individual legislators and those adopted by NCOIL.

For example, some insurance commissioners have recently taken action to require insurers to be much more sensitive to the effects of climate change on their solvency and underwriting practices.[34] Yet quite a few legislators consider that to be an example of excessive govern-

---

[31] https://content.naic.org/state-insurance-departments (last visited July 11, 2023).

[32] http://www.naic.org/prod_serv_publications.htm (last visited July 11, 2023).

[33] http://33a.fce.mwp.acessdomain.com (last visited July 11, 2023).

[34] *See, e.g.,* https://www.insurance.ca.gov/01-consumers/180-climate -change/; https://content.naic.org/article/us-insurance-commissioners-endorse

ment intrusion into the operations of private businesses in a free market economy. NCOIL itself, unlike the NAIC, has taken no position on how insurers should address climate change, if at all. Nevertheless, at an NCOIL meeting in 2022 several insurance commissioners discussed this topic with legislators, including the activities of the various NAIC committees, such as the NAIC National Climate and Resiliency Task Force, dealing with this issue. Through such periodic dialogue between commissioners and legislators at the three NCOIL meetings each year, harmful misconceptions can be avoided, and both the executive and legislative branches can work more harmoniously to fashion and implement sound regulation.

In 2022 NCOIL was working on drafting a model law that, if adopted by a state, would authorize that state's insurance department to establish a "regulatory sandbox". In recent years states have toyed with the idea of permitting companies in the "insurtech" space to receive temporary waivers from laws which would otherwise prohibit or restrict useful innovations, such as, for example, a property/casualty insurance policy of very limited duration. Hence the term "regulatory sandbox" has come into vogue. Chapter 9 discusses the regulatory issues arising from the burgeoning use of "insurtech".

BOX 3.3   PRACTICAL TIPS FOR PRACTITIONERS

The following are useful periodical publications about U.S. insurance regulation:

- *NAIC Newswire* (daily) (free e-mail subscription) https://naicforum .naic.org/comnewswire.htm (last visited July 11, 2023)
- Federation of Regulatory Counsel Journals (free access) https://www.forc.org/Public/Journal/Public/Journals/Welcome _to_FORC_Journals.aspx?hkey=938a4f8f-56cf-4021-8141 -6f0dcfdad64c (last visited July 11, 2023)
- *Business Insurance* (paid subscription)

For many questions you will first want to determine which U.S.

-internationally-recognized-climate-risk-disclosure-standard (last visited July 11, 2023).

state is the domicile of an insurance company and/or which U.S. state is applying, or may apply, its laws to an insurance regulatory issue. If you are not admitted to practice in that particular state, your client(s) may need you to coordinate the provision of advice from counsel admitted and practicing in each particular state involved. The three principal sources of U.S. state insurance regulations are:

- the state statute, e.g. the New York Insurance Law or the California Insurance Code, codifying the various laws governing the organization and operation of insurance companies and insurance professionals;
- the regulations issued by the state insurance department; and
- any informal guidance issued by that department, such as bulletins, advisories, or Circular Letters in New York, along with, in New York, informal published opinions of the Office of General Counsel of the New York Insurance Department from 2000 through 2010.

Today almost all websites of U.S. state insurance departments provide links to the statutes and regulations which they administer, and most, if not all, informal guidance issued by that department is accessible right on the website.

4. How states define what "insurance" is and who is an insurer, and how states license insurance companies and insurance professionals

Every state in the United States requires an insurance company to be licensed either in that state if it does an insurance business there, or in its domicile for surplus line or excess line placements. (These placements are discussed *infra* at pp. 63 to 66) Moreover, every state requires anyone who *sells*, *solicits*, or *negotiates* an insurance policy to a person located in the state to be licensed as an insurance agent, insurance broker, or insurance producer, depending on the applicable terminology in that state's law. Before focusing on the processes and procedures that state insurance departments use for licensing insurers, producers, and other insurance professionals, we should consider how states define "insurance" to determine if a person or entity legally needs to be licensed there.

I. WHAT IS "INSURANCE" AND WHO IS AN INSURER?

1. How States Define "Insurance"

Most states have a statutory definition of what constitutes an insurance contract.[1] "A contract of insurance is an agreement by which one party for a consideration promises to pay money or its equivalent, or to do an act valuable to the insured, upon the destruction, loss or injury of something in which the other party has an interest."

> "Insurance contract" means any agreement or other transaction whereby one party, the "insurer", is obligated to confer benefit of pecuniary value upon another party, the "insured" or "beneficiary", dependent upon the happening

---

[1]   *See, e.g.,* Mass. G.L. ch. 175, Sec. 2.

of a fortuitous event in which the insured or beneficiary has, or is expected to have at the time of such happening, a material interest which will be adversely affected by the happening of such event... "Fortuitous event" means any occurrence or failure to occur which is, or is assumed by the parties to be, to a substantial extent beyond the control of either party.[2]

Some states do not have statutory definitions of the term "insurance", but, rather, utilize definitions derived from decided cases at common law. For example, the Tex. Ins. Code § 101.051(b) lists certain specified activities as constituting "the business of insurance" but contains no statutory definition of the term "insurance" itself, unlike many other states. Instead, Texas courts have grappled with the question of whether a particular transaction or arrangements constitutes insurance, for which a license is legally required.[3] In these cases, courts consider closely the overall purpose of the arrangement or transaction, the degree to which risk distribution or risk spreading has occurred, if at all, and whether the insured person or entity has separately paid a specific premium for the protection being offered.[4]

2. States Do NOT Treat Most Warranties, Guarantees, Contractual Damage Waivers, and Service Contracts on Products, and Some Debt Cancellation Agreements, As Insurance

A. Warranties, guarantees and service contracts

Although states broadly define the term "insurance" to require licensure and regulation of most indemnitors who incur the risk of loss if fortuitous events occur, for very practical reasons state insurance laws are careful to exclude from the definition of "insurance" many persons and entities who, by contract, would otherwise come within the broad definition of "insurance". For example, the New York Insurance Law expressly excepts those who make guaranties and warranties as an "incidental" part of their main legitimate business, and who, or which, do not issue those guarantees and warranties as a vocation.[5] Otherwise, every time a parent

---

[2] *See also*, N.Y. Ins. L. § 1101.
[3] *Texas Dep't of Ins. v. Am. Nat. Ins. Co.*, 410 S.W.3d 843 (Tex. 2012); *In re Texas Ass'n. of School Boards, Inc.*, 169 S.W.3d 653, 658 (Tex. 2005).
[4] *See also*: *Griffin Systems, Inc. v. Washburn*, 505 N.E.2d 1121 (Ill. App. Ct. 1987
[5] N.Y. Ins. L. § 1101(b)(1).

company issues a guarantee to a person or entity entering a contract with a subsidiary that the parent will guarantee performance of the subsidiary's obligations in that contract, the parent company would have to be licensed as an insurance company. Similarly, if that exception were not in the law, every time a manufacturer made a warranty that an automobile, or a computer or an air conditioner which it manufactured would be replaced or repaired if defective, the manufacturer would have to be licensed as an insurance company.

In 1938 the New York Court of Appeals, that state's highest court, issued a seminal decision in *Ollendorff Watch Co. v. Pink*,[6] which differentiated between a manufacturer's warranty and a contract of insurance. To induce consumers to buy their watches during the Depression, the watch company advertised that if its watch were stolen during the first year of ownership, the company would replace the watch. The New York State Superintendent of Insurance, Louis Pink, asserted it was doing an unlicensed insurance business. The Court of Appeals agreed, stating that, in contrast to an insurance policy covering theft, "a warranty would relate in some way to the nature or efficiency of the product sold—in this case, that the watch would work or was of a certain make and fineness. A warranty would not cover a hazard having nothing whatever to do with the make or quality of the watch."[7] By contrast, the United States Court of Appeals for the Fourth Circuit applied this principle in holding that a manufacturer's warranty covering a heating and ventilation system was a warranty, and not insurance, even though it offered to repair or replace a defective system damaged by inclement weather which was obviously a fortuitous event.[8]

In a majority of U.S. states, a manufacturer's or seller's warranty as to the quality of the product made or sold does not constitute an insurance policy if the warranty is not issued for a separate price. These states, however, have adopted service contract laws which specifically exempt

---

[6]   279 N.Y. 32 (1938).
[7]   279 N.Y. at 36.
[8]   *GAF Corp. v. County School Bd.*, 629 F.2d 981 (4th Cir. 1980); *but see: Griffin Systems, Inc. v. Washburn*, 505 N.E.2d 1121 (III.App.Ct. 1987); *Riffe v. Home Finders Associates, Inc.*, 205 W. Va. 216, 220 (W. Va. 1999); *Guaranteed Warranty Corp., Inc. v. State ex rel. Humphrey*, 23 Ariz. App. 327 (Ariz. App. 1975) (so-called "service contracts" issued by entities that did *not* manufacture or sell the covered products and which indemnified consumers if car or home needed repair held to be insurance).

extended warranties or service contracts—sold for a separate price—from regulation as insurance policies.[9] Under these state service contract laws, anyone who issues service contracts, colloquially known as "extended warranties", for a separate price must be duly registered with the state agency which regulates service contracts, usually the state insurance department, even if the issuer of the service contract manufactured the covered product. (In California the Department of Consumer Affairs and in Texas the Department of Licensing and Regulation are the pertinent agencies.) To ensure that service contract providers have the financial resources to perform the product repair or replacement obligations stated in the service contracts they have issued, registration typically requires establishment of a funded reserve account, or purchase of a service contract reimbursement insurance policy from a licensed insurer, or having a net worth, or having a parent company with a net worth, which exceeds a specified minimum amount, such as $100 million.[10]

B.   Storage damage and collision damage waivers

Courts in California and New York have ruled that provisions in car rental and self-storage agreements which shift the risk of damage for fortuitous events from one party to another are not insurance policies, so that the party assuming the risk need not legally be a licensed insurer, even though that party is charging the customer a specific amount for that protection. Thus, in *Heckart v. A-1 Self Storage Inc.*,[11] the California Supreme Court held that a self-storage contract which provided that, in return for a specified fee, the self-storage company would assume the risk of damage to the self-storage unit if a fire or other fortuitous event occurs was *not* an insurance policy, and the self-storage company was not legally required to be a licensed insurance company. The Court focused on the overall purpose of the transaction, i.e. the rental of a storage unit, as distinct from the purpose of an insurance policy which is to transfer and distribute risk among multiple insureds.

---

[9] *See, e.g.,* Nev. R.S. 690C.010 *et seq.*; Tex. Occ. Code Ch. 1304.
[10] *See, e.g.,* N.Y. Ins. L. § 7903.
[11] 4 Cal 5th 749 (Cal. 2018).

Similarly, in *Truta v. Avis Rent A Car System*,[12] *Klein v. National Car Rental*[13] (and *Hertz Corp. v. Corcoran*,[14]) California and New York courts held that rental car collision damage waivers, under which rental car companies agreed, for a separate fee, to waive property damage claims if the renter were involved in an accident, were *not* insurance contracts. The overall purpose of the transaction was to rent a car, not to spread risk.

C.   Debt cancellation or suspension agreements

The federal office of the Comptroller of the Currency has ruled that national banks may offer debt cancellation agreements to borrowers, under which debt service is cancelled or suspended, if, e.g. the borrower dies or becomes disabled, and no state licensure of the lender as an insurance company is required. This rule has been upheld as not subject to reverse preemption under the McCarran-Ferguson Act, given the broad powers afforded national banks by Congress.[15]

On the other hand, a lender which is *not* a national bank which offers a similar feature to borrowers must be licensed as an insurer, at least in New York, and, depending on how their courts construe the definition of "insurance", in other states as well. A New York court ruled, and the New York State Insurance Department twice opined, that a lender which was not a national bank and which offered to waive certain debt service payments if the borrower became disabled, was, in fact, doing an insurance business for which licensure as an insurance company was legally required.[16]

---

[12]   193 Cal.App.3d 802 (Ct. App. 1987).
[13]   N.Y. Supreme Ct., Spec. Term, May 4, 1983) No. 227 20/822082, affd. 100 A.D. 2d 987 (1st Dept. 1984), *lv. app. den.*, 63 N.Y. 2d 605.
[14]   137 Misc. 2d 403 (N.Y. Sup. Ct. 1987).
[15]   *First National Bank of Eastern Arkansas v. Taylor*, 907 F.2d 775 (8th Cir. 1990).
[16]   *Luc Leasing Inc. v. Muhl*, 172 Misc. 2d 753 (Sup. Ct. 1997); https://www .dfs.ny.gov/insurance/ogco2002/rg205031.htm (last visited July 11, 2023).

3. A Person or Entity Required to be Licensed does Not Need to be Physically Present in a State for the Licensure Requirement to Apply

In the U.S. the concept of "long-arm" regulatory jurisdiction is a well-established feature of state insurance regulation. Over 80 years ago the U.S. Supreme Court ruled that it was constitutional for a state to subject an out-of-state insurance company to regulation if it mailed insurance policies to persons located in that state, even if the company had no offices there. *Hoopeston Canning Co. v. Cullen.*[17] More recent cases have ruled that states can constitutionally regulate out-of-state insurers which solicited persons in the state to buy insurance policies or which engaged adjusters in the state to quantify damage claims, even if the company had no officers or employees in the state.[18]

4. An Insurance Company that has No Offices, No Agents, No Bank Accounts in a State, and uses No Adjusters in that State—as of Now—Need Not be Licensed there

In the very rare situation where an insurance company has no offices, no agents, and no bank accounts in a state, and utilizes no adjusters there to evaluate damage claims, that insurer, as of now, would likely *not* be required to hold a license from that state. The U.S. Supreme Court considered such a scenario in *State Bd. of Ins. v. Todd Shipyards Corp.*[19] The Court held that under the Due Process Clause of the Fourteenth Amendment Texas could not apply its premium tax law to an insurer which did not solicit in Texas, did not issue or deliver policies there, did not accept premium payments there, and did not adjust losses there.

Note: that the facts in *Todd* Shipyards are very unusual, and later cases have questioned its continued vitality.

---

[17] 318 U.S. 313 (1943).
[18] *Associated Electric & Gas Insurance Services Ltd v. R. Gary Clark*, 676 A.2d 1357 (Sup. Ct. R.I. 1996). (where Bermuda insurer systematically adjusted losses in Rhode Island, insurer could be subject to that state's regulations even though policies were issued and delivered in Bermuda); *Haisten v. Grass Valley Medical Reimbursement Fund*, 784 F.2d 1392 (9th Cir. 1986) (where insurer purposefully solicited prospective policyholders in California, that state could constitutionally apply its insurer licensing laws even though policies were issued and delivered outside of California).
[19] 370 U.S. 451 (1962).

5.   Direct Procurement of Insurance Policies by Insureds

It is not illegal, as a matter of constitutional law under the *Todd Shipyards*
case, for an unlicensed insurance company to simply insure property
or casualty risks in a state if it does NOT advertise, negotiate the terms
of coverage, issue policies, deliver policies, collect premium, contract
with agents, or adjust claims in that state, and has no office in that state.
The insurer can legally issue and deliver a policy to a policyholder who
travels to the state or country in which the insurer is licensed for the particular kind of insurance involved and negotiates the policy terms, pays
for the policy, and obtains the policy there.

When a policyholder does that, the process is called "direct procurement". In many states, such as New York, the unlicensed insurer may
legally mail premium bills and related correspondence to a "direct procurement" policyholder, as long as the policy is "principally negotiated,
issued and delivered" in a jurisdiction in which the insurer is licensed for
the same kind of insurance.[20] The policyholder may be liable to her, his
or its state taxing authorities for a "direct procurement" tax which is like
a use tax.[21]

6.   Internet Sales of Insurance

As to internet sales of insurance, state regulators focus on the extent to
which the consumer interacts with a business' web page. Merely posting
a web advertisement that is visible to a person located in a state where the
business lacks the requisite license is probably not actionable, although it
would be advisable for the web page to indicate that the insurance is "not
available in all states".

However, communicating with a consumer who has clicked on
a solicitation will be considered doing business in the state in which the
consumer is located, whether or not insurance is actually sold; and the
business doing the communicating must have the requisite license(s) in
the state(s) in which the consumer is located.[22]

---

[20]   *See, e.g.,* N.Y. Ins. L. § 1102(b)(2)(E).
[21]   *See, e.g.,* Alabama Code § 27-10-35(c).
[22]   *See, e.g.,* N.Y. Dept. of Fin. Serv., Opinion of General Counsel, March 6,
2000 accessible at: https://www.dfs.ny.gov/insurance/ogco2000/rg000362.htm
(last visited July 11, 2023).

BOX 4.1   PRACTICAL TIPS FOR PRACTITIONERS

If a client is not a licensed insurer but wants to offer protection against loss to a contractual counterparty anywhere in the U.S., carefully review the statutory and/or common law definition of "insurance" in *each* state in which the client wants to operate. Do NOT assume that every state will have the same position as to whether the proposed transaction or arrangement constitutes insurance for which licensure is required.

Because state insurance regulators are reluctant to say if a proposed course of action is legal or illegal, especially in a phone call or virtual meeting, ask the regulator whether her or his agency has taken enforcement action in the past against a person or entity who or which has done something similar to what your client would like to offer in that state, and, if so, how public documents about that proceeding can be acquired. That line of inquiry is much more likely to elicit useful information than simply asking an Insurance Department official—who probably would not be authorized to render legal opinions—if your client's proposal is permissible.

If you are advising an insurance company client which does not wish to be licensed in a state, and does not wish to qualify as an approved surplus line or excess line insurer, in order to come within the *Todd Shipyards* doctrine, that client must:

(1)   avoid discussing terms and conditions of coverage with anyone located in that state in person or by mail, email, phone, virtual electronic meetings, or text—instead insisting that the prospective purchaser come to a jurisdiction in which the client is licensed to underwrite that line of insurance to have that discussion;

(2)   avoid sending any written or electronic solicitation, by any means of communication, to anyone located in that state to purchase a policy;

(3)   avoid sending any policy, certificate or other evidence of coverage to anyone in that state by any means of communication;

(4)   avoid receiving premium or depositing premium in an account of a bank or other financial institution located in that state;

(5)   avoid hiring any adjusters in that state to evaluate losses and claims; and

(6)   avoid directing any print or electronic advertising specifically to persons located in that state.

II.   HOW STATES LICENSE INSURANCE COMPANIES AND INSURANCE PROFESSIONALS

1.   Commercial Insurance Companies

States in the U.S. utilize a set of application forms developed by the NAIC to evaluate applications for licensure as insurance companies. These are combined into a filing called the "Uniform Certificate of Authority Application" and can be seen on the NAIC website at: http://www.naic.org/industry_ucaa.htm (last visited July 11, 2023). Note the difference between the "primary" and "expansion" applications. A "Primary" application is filed by an entity as its INITIAL application in state of domicile. Once that company has been "admitted" or licensed in its domicile, depending on the length of time it has profitably operated in its domicile, it may file additional applications—called "Expansion" applications—in other U.S. states to be "admitted" there.

Each Primary and Expansion application is lengthy, complicated, and includes numerous documents demonstrating the financial viability, the expertise in operating a profitable insurance company, and the personal competence and sterling integrity of the applicant's directors and officers. All U.S. states consider the following key elements in both a Primary and all Expansion applications:

First, the application must contain a *sound, detailed, and credible business plan*, keyed to that state, accompanied by financial projections, usually for three years, showing credible projections for premium income, allocated and unallocated expenses, loss reserves, unearned premium reserves, reinsurance ceded and assumed, investment income, and other financial data. Typically, applicants retain expert actuaries and accountants to prepare these required *pro forma* financial projections.

Second, the applicant must meet required *capital and surplus levels*—to support the proposed business plan—which almost always are considerably more than relatively low statutory minimum amounts.

Third, the applicant must present *director and officer biographical affidavits* which detail the educational and vocational background of the officers and directors of the applicant company. The affidavits require the affiant who signs the affidavit under penalty of criminal perjury to indicate in detail any professional or occupational license suspensions or revocations, any governmental regulatory investigations, and any criminal convictions (other than routine traffic tickets). A copy of the standard biographical affidavit developed by the NAIC can be accessed at: https://content.naic.org/sites/default/files/inline-files/industry_ucaa_form11.pdf (last visited July 11, 2023).

Most states require that every single item in a biographical affidavit be independently verified by an approved third-party verification service.

Fourth, each applicant must obtain regulatory approval for the name it wishes to use in that state, which cannot be so close to a previously approved name as to cause confusion among consumers and the public.[23]

Fifth, the licensing state may require that the applicant fund a deposit account at a licensed bank or trust company, with the state insurance commissioner (or equivalent official) authorized to make withdrawals to cover the insurer's liabilities. Deposits are typically required for insurance companies writing workers' compensation business.

Sixth, an insurer may be required to agree in writing that it will comply with particular state laws, such as N.Y. Ins. L. 1106 which prohibits licensed insurers domiciled outside of New York from doing *anywhere* any kind of insurance business which a New York domestic insurer may not legally do. California has a similar extra-territorial law which prohibits a licensed insurer, even if domiciled outside of California, from merging or consolidating without first obtaining regulatory approval.[24]

Before licensing an insurer, state insurance regulators check to make sure the company has been properly organized and registered with the Secretary of State's office as either a domestic company or as a foreign company. They also determine the Certificate of Incorporation or other charter document, and any company by-laws, are in proper form. Moreover, they make sure that each domestic company has the requisite number and identity of directors.[25]

Alien insurers, which are domiciled outside of the U.S., file a "primary application" with a particular state insurance department to be admitted

---

[23] *See, e.g.,* https://www.dfs.ny.gov/apps_and_licensing/entity_name_approval (last visited July 11, 2023) and N.Y. Bus. Corp. L. § 301(a)(5)(B).

[24] Cal. Ins. Code 1011(c).

[25] *See, e.g.,* N.Y. Ins. L. §§ 1201, 1202 (requiring at least seven directors for domestic insurers, at least one of whom must be a New York resident, a majority of whom must be U.S. citizens and residents, and, for life insurers, one-third of whom must be "independent", i.e. not employed by that company or parent or subsidiary/affiliate.)

as a "U.S. Branch" in that state as the "state of entry". They must agree
in writing to be amenable to suit in the courts of that state, and they must
also establish a trust fund in a U.S. licensed bank or trust company with
the Insurance Commissioner (or equivalent state official) as named beneficiary of the trust account. The amount to be held in trust is typically
negotiated between the applicant (and its counsel) and the insurance
regulators in that state but will cover all the alien insurer's projected U.S.
liabilities for losses, expenses, and unearned premiums.

If an insurance company is owned, controlled or subsidized by
a foreign country government, some U.S. states impose specific prohibitions and requirements. *See e.g.* Cal. Ins. Code 699.5 (before issuing
a license Commissioner must consider if: the insurer would receive an
unfair subsidy from foreign government, if a foreign government will
exert undue influence over insurer, if insurer could assert sovereign
immunity defense to suits, if the insurer would discriminate on the
basis of race, religion, or national origin, and if the insurer has adequate
security measures in place to protect confidentiality of non-public information. Note, no insurer "*wholly owned*" by a foreign government can be
licensed in California).

For "Expansion" applications a key element is acceptable proof of
a three-year track record of profitability as a licensed company in at
least one other state —the so-called "seasoning" requirement. Applicants
must file copies, or provide access to, all their filed quarterly and annual
financial statements for the preceding three years to show the required
length of profitability. This "seasoning" requirement can be waived
under certain circumstances, e.g., a sister company or subsidiary of
the applicant is already licensed in the state, or the applicant is a new
company created to satisfy an urgent market need for a particular type
of insurance—which is usually arranged in coordination with the same
insurance department which will evaluate the application.[26]

For Expansion applications, besides acceptable proof of "seasoning",
a credible business plan, sound financial projections, and the detailed,
independently verified biographical affidavits of the applicant's officers
and directors, all states also require:

• *certificates of good standing* from insurance departments in every
  state in which the applicant insurer is currently licensed;

---

[26]   *See, e.g.,* Fla. Stat. § 624.404.

- a detailed description of the applicant's current or proposed reinsurance program, both as to cessions and assumptions;
- copies (in some states certified) of any *reports on examination* prepared by any other insurance departments and *copies of previously filed financial statements*; and
- copies of all documents arising from any enforcement actions and proceedings against the applicant initiated by any other state insurance officials.

States have enacted "retaliatory" laws to ensure that their domestic insurers are not disadvantaged when competing against insurers domiciled in other states or a foreign country.[27] As part of the licensing process, insurers submitting Expansion applications must agree that if their domestic state has higher taxes and fees that would be imposed on insurers domiciled in the state in which they seek to be licensed, then they will pay the licensing state taxes and fees at that same higher rate.

Although the UCAA process is intended to be quite similar among the various states, it is important to note that there are still numerous variations in required procedures. For example, different states will have different rules for items such as required submission of fingerprints for the company's directors and officers with some states, such as New York, notorious in demanding fingerprints. (The New York State Insurance Department many years ago required a former President of the United States, who did not resign, to submit fingerprints when he was a director of an insurer). Other states require that proposed policy forms and/or in-force reinsurance agreements be filed as part of an Expansion application. The UCAA web pages list these various state variations.[28]

BOX 4.2 PRACTICAL TIPS FOR PRACTITIONERS ADVISING ENTITIES SEEKING LICENSURE

First, retain expert U.S. counsel who have practiced for years in the state in which your client is applying for admission. These lawyers should be known to, and highly respected by, the state insurance regu-

---

[27] *See, e.g.,* Cal. Ins. Code § 685 and N.Y. Ins. L. § 1112.
[28] https://content.naic.org/industry/ucaa; https://content.naic.org/industry_ucaa_chart_fingerprint_bio_affidavit.htm (last visited July 11, 2023).

lators who will evaluate your client's application.
  Second, advise your client to

(a) be prepared to travel to the state for an introductory and then
     several subsequent in-person meetings with those state insurance
     regulators and
(b) be prepared for a lengthy process requiring concessions as to its
     proposed business plan, the amount of capital and policyholder
     surplus it must hold, and the type of written commitments it must
     make to the regulators, for its application to be approved.

2.   When a Licensed Insurance Company Wants to Write More Lines of Business in a State

Sometimes an insurer that is already licensed in a state to issue one or
more kinds of insurance wants to be allowed to issue a different kind of
insurance. The insurer will submit a "corporate amendment" application
using the same UCAA process which it used to become licensed in that
state initially. The process typically is not as long or complicated as the
initial licensing process, but the states do require the insurer to submit
valid fiscal and actuarial projections showing how premiums, expenses
and reserves would not be adversely affected if the insurer is granted the
additional writing authority.[29]

3.   When a Licensed Insurance Company Domiciled in One State Wants to Re-domesticate to Another State

For business reasons or because its corporate parent has changed,
a domestic insurance company sometimes wants to re-domesticate to
another state. If the company is licensed to write the same kinds of insurance in its new home state, and if both the current state and the new state
have both enacted the NAIC Model Redomestication Act, the procedure
is relatively simple: an application for re-domestication must be filed

---

[29] https://www.naic.org/documents/industry_ucaa_corp_amend.pdf#:~:text
=The%20Corporate%20Amendment%20Application%20of%20the%20UCAA
%20provides,Applications%20within%2060%20calendar%20%20days%20of
%20receipt.   https://www.naic.org/documents/industry_ucaa_user_guide_corp
_amend.pdf?100 (last visited July 11, 2023).

in both states indicating the reasons for the re-domestication and what additional changes, if any, the insurer wants to undertake. Regulators in both states must approve the application for the re-domestication to take effect, but unless the company is currently being examined by the domestic state or there is some concern over its financial condition, those approvals are almost always granted. In states which have adopted the NAIC Model, the company remains the same and does not need to merge or consolidate with any other company, while enjoying all the rights, and having to comply with all of the obligations, of a domestic company in the new domicile. The NAIC Model Redomestication Act can be accessed here: https://content.naic.org/sites/default/files/MO350 .pdf (last visited July 11, 2023).

It is critical to note that not every U.S. state has adopted the NAIC Model. For example, a New York domestic insurer wishing to re-domesticate will need to effect a merger with a company organized and already licensed in the new domicile and obtain approval of both the New York Superintendent of Financial Services and the insurance commissioner, or equivalent official, of the new domicile. *See* New York Insurance Law, Article 71.

In 1998 a licensed New York domestic insurer in excellent financial condition filed a merger agreement, duly approved by the Board of Directors of both companies under Article 71, with both the then New York Superintendent of Insurance and the Michigan Insurance Commissioner. The merger agreement accompanied an application to re-domesticate to Michigan, where the insurer's parent company had its principal office, and become a licensed foreign insurer in New York, writing the same kinds of insurance it had been writing as a licensed New York domestic insurer in good standing for close to 75 years. The staff of the New York Insurance Department nevertheless insisted that the company undergo the full licensing process before the re-domestication could take effect, even though no changes at all would occur in operations, finances, and leadership of the insurance company—only that the domicile would change. After efforts to negotiate with staff proved fruitless, it took a call from the Michigan Insurance Commissioner to the New York Superintendent of Insurance to personally request expedited approval of the application for the re-domestication to occur. It helped that both regulators were appointed by Governors of the same political party and that the insurer was a wholly-owned subsidiary of one of the world's leading automobile manufacturers with dealers in every county of New York State. The New York Superintendent instantly recognized the political ramifications if the re-domestication were delayed while the company underwent the full licensing process.

> ## BOX 4.3   PRACTICAL TIP FOR PRACTITIONERS
>
> Whether or not one or both of the states involved in a redomestication have enacted the NAIC Model Redomestication Act, it will be necessary to retain counsel known to, and respected by, both insurance departments, either one counsel, or two if the same counsel is not experienced in dealing with regulators at both departments. Counsel should arrange at least two in-person meetings with the relevant decision-makers at both insurance departments, and the general counsel and CFO of the insurer should attend both meetings to explain the reason(s) for re-domesticating and answer any questions department staff may have.

4.   "Captive" Insurance Companies

Many Fortune 500 companies, and even smaller ones, have established "captive" insurance companies as subsidiaries to cover the risks of the parent company and any subsidiaries and/or affiliates, and the business risks of their officers and directors and employees. Captives are almost always licensed only in the domestic state, even though they may insure property and casualty risks located in other states. Vermont, South Carolina, Hawaii, and Utah are among the leading captive domiciles in the U.S., with Bermuda serving as the main offshore domicile. Captives usually directly insure a small layer of risk of the parent company and/or affiliates and subsidiaries (and their personnel) and then find reinsurers to assume the much larger amounts of risk.

To become licensed in the domestic state, a captive must file a sensible business plan and appoint an approved captive management firm with substantial experience in managing captives, as well as file biographical affidavits on its directors and officers. U.S. insurance regulators have traditionally viewed captives as a form of self-insurance if the captive is not insuring unaffiliated third parties. So, even though a captive only licensed in Vermont may deliver a policy to its parent company in Massachusetts, regulators in Massachusetts have not sought to enjoin or penalize the

transaction because they consider it to be self-insurance and not transact-
ing insurance for third parties. Other state insurance departments take the
same position.

5.   Risk Retention Groups Organized under the Federal Liability Risk Retention Act of 1986

In the 1980s businesses and some professionals encountered difficulty
in obtaining affordable liability insurance covering damages owed in
tort, contract and breach of fiduciary duty. Congress therefore enacted
the Liability Risk Retention Act.[30] This statute specifically preempts
any state insurance licensing law and allows persons and entities in
the same trade or profession to join together to create a *liability risk
retention group* (RRG) covering the liability risks of its members. Only
liability risks may be covered. An RRG may *not* insure property, provide
workers' compensation insurance, or provide life or health insurance.

An RRG must be licensed in at least one state or the District of
Columbia, and licensure is heavily dependent on the quality and level
of detail in a feasibility study which it must submit as the key part of its
license application. The study must cover projected premiums, losses,
expenses, investments, and reinsurance and marketing arrangements,
among other topics. The study must include credible actuarial projections
on losses and reserves from a qualified actuary. Once the RRG is licensed
in one U.S. jurisdiction, it may operate in every other state by filing
a registration statement, submitting a copy of the feasibility study used
to obtain licensure in its domestic state, and a copy of an annual financial
statement issued by a certified public accountant along with an opinion
on its reserves from a qualified actuary or loss reserve specialist, if it has
already been in operation.[31]

An RRG legally operating in a state must still comply with all state
laws which have not been preempted, such as a state unfair claims
practices act. A state may seek to enjoin operation of an RRG which has
sold, or seeks to sell, coverage for a person or entity not eligible to be
a member, e.g., not being in the same trade, business or profession as
the RRG members, or if the RRG is in a hazardous financial condition.[32]

---

[30]   15 U.S.C. § 3901 *et seq.* (LRRA).
[31]   15 U.S.C. § 3902.
[32]   15 U.S.C. § 3902.

6.   Licensing Insurance Professionals

A.   Agents, brokers, producers

States require licenses for insurance agents, insurance brokers, and insurance producers if denominated as such in the state insurance code. States differentiate between "individual" licenses for persons and "business entity" licenses for corporations, partnerships, and limited liability companies, etc. Licensure of individuals almost always requires undertaking a mandated pre-licensing course and successfully passing a written examination, unless, depending on the state, the applicant has already received a specified professional designation, e.g., CPCU (Chartered Property Casualty Underwriter). Most states impose continuing education requirements on *resident* individual licensees, and some require fingerprinting. An applicant licensed in good standing in her or his or its state of residence can obtain a non-resident license to sell the same line or lines of insurance as is, or are, permitted by the resident license.[33]

Most states have adopted a common definition for acting as an insurance producer—either an agent or a broker—for which licensure by that state is legally required. "Insurance producer" means a person required to be licensed under the laws of this state to *sell, solicit* or *negotiate* insurance.[34] A list of all of the states which adopted the Producer Licensing Model Act can be found at the end of the Model Act.[35]

Almost all states now use the Uniform Application for Individual Producer License/Registration and the Uniform Application for Business Entity License/Registration developed by the NAIC. To streamline the licensing process for agents and brokers who do business in multiple states, the National Insurance Producer Registry (NIPR) is an electronic portal developed by the NAIC that allows a resident licensee to apply for and renew producer licenses as a non-resident in all other states without having to separately file the applications. Its website is: https://pdb.nipr .com/my-nipr/frontend/identify-licensee (last visited July 11, 2023).

Note that a business entity must designate at least one "Designated Responsible Licensed Producer" as its regulatory compliance officer who must be individually licensed in that state as a resident or as

---

[33]   *See, e.g.,* N.Y. Ins. L. §§ 2101–2108.

[34]   NAIC Producer Licensing Model Act, Section 2. D. https://content.naic .org/sites/default/files/inline-files/MDL-218.pdf (last visited July 11, 2023).

[35]   *See, e.g.,* Mass. G.L., ch. 175, § 162l; 215 ILCS 5/500-10; Iowa Ins. Code 522B.1 adopting Model Act definition.

a non-resident for the same line of insurance as the business entity wishes to sell. Some states, such as North Dakota, require a DRLP to be an officer, partner or LLC member of the business entity, and others do not. In New York the DRLP is called a "sub-licensee" who must be an officer or employee of the business entity. States require licensed persons to promptly report changes of address and any revocations, suspensions, fines, or other disciplinary penalties imposed by another state. Some states, like Pennsylvania, go so far as to require a producer to provide that information if a parent company or affiliate is disciplined in another jurisdiction or sanctioned by a federal agency such as the U.S. Securities and Exchange Commission.

Besides being properly licensed to sell particular kinds of insurance, agents must also be *appointed by the insurers they represent*. State insurance departments leave it up to the insurance companies which licensed agents should be appointed, but most do require that a "certificate of appointment" be filed within 15 days of the inception of an agency contract or the first application for insurance is submitted.[36]

Depending on the state, however, there are important exceptions to producer licensing requirements. For example, employees of insurance companies or insurance producers who are only paid a salary and who do not receive commissions are not required to be licensed in most states.[37] Employees of businesses, which purchase group life and/or health insurance, who obtain and furnish information and assist in administration for the purpose of enrolling employees in group insurance programs, are not required to be licensed, *provided* that these persons do not receive a commission for their administrative activities.[38]

Also not required to be licensed in New York and other states are persons who only refer other persons to licensed producers *and* who (i) do not receive any compensation based on the sale of insurance and (ii) do not discuss the specific terms and conditions of insurance.[39] Employees and authorized salespersons of portable electronics vendors, self-storage businesses, travel agencies and rental car companies, can legally avoid licensure, *provided* that such persons undertake required

---

[36] *See, e.g.,* N.Y. Ins. L. § 2112; Nev. R.S. § 683A.321.
[37] *See, e.g.,* Mass. G.L., ch. 175, § 162J(b)(1).
[38] *See, e.g.,* Maine Insurance Code § 1420-C.
[39] *See, e.g.,* N.Y. Ins. L. Sec. 2114.

training and make available required consumer brochures as specified in the applicable statute.[40]

B.   Managing general agents

States license and regulate *managing general agents* (MGAs). An MGA is a person or business entity who manages all or part of the underwriting of policies under contract with a licensed insurer, and pays claims, binds reinsurance, or, in a state such as Maryland, maintains the insurer's loss reserves. MGAs often deal with "retail agents" who, in turn, deal directly with the policyholder. Insurance companies delegate the power to underwrite policies, i.e., decide if the policy should be issued and for what amounts, to managing general agents by contract.

Because each MGA has enormous power to affect the finances of the contracting insurance company by deciding what risks to underwrite, and because in the 1980s several large insurers became insolvent resulting from fraud and embezzlement by MGAs, the NAIC adopted the Model Managing General Agents Act regulating their conduct.[41]

Every state has adopted a version of this Model Act as a condition of being an "accredited NAIC state".[42] These laws require that contracts between an MGA and the insurer contain specified provisions, such as, e.g., the insurer's right to terminate the contract for cause, the underwriting standards which the MGA must follow, the requirement that the MGA be audited by a certified public accountant, the requirement that the insurer conduct periodic examinations of the MGA, the requirement that the MGA remit premium and render accounts to the insurer timely, the conditions under which the MGA is allowed to pay claims under the insurance policies, the prohibition on the MGA binding the insurer to assume reinsurance, and the prohibition on the MGA serving as a director of the insurer without regulatory approval.

---

[40]   *See, e.g.,* Mass. G.L., ch. 175, § 162Y; N.Y. Ins. L. § 2131; Pennsylvania Statutes Title 40 P.S. Insurance § 4604.

[41]   https://content.naic.org/sites/default/files/inline-files/MDL-225.pdf   (last visited July 11, 2023).

[42]   *See, e.g.,* Tenn. Code Ann. §§ 56-6-501 to 56-6-510; Neb. Rev. Stat. §§ 44-4901 to 44-4910; Md. Ins. Code Ann. §§ 8-201 to 8-213; Mass. G.L. ch. 175, §§ 177G to 177L.

C.   Adjusters

States license and regulate *adjusters*. An adjuster who is paid by an insurer to evaluate and determine claims on its behalf is known as an "independent adjuster", while an adjuster who is paid by a policyholder or claimant to negotiate over a claim with an insurer (or the insurer's independent adjuster) is called a "public adjuster".[43] Depending on the state, employees of insurers, licensed attorneys and under specified conditions licensed agents, among others, are exempt from adjuster licensing requirements.[44]

As with producers, in most states applicants for adjuster licenses must submit biographical information, complete a pre-licensing course and pass an examination.[45] Some states require that the applicant furnish an acceptable surety bond and fingerprints.

D.   Third-party administrators

States license and regulate *third-party administrators* (TPAs). A TPA is a person or business which processes, evaluates and pays life and health insurance claims—typically for a self-funded employer or union health plan—somewhat similarly to how an adjuster handles property-casualty claims. Like an adjuster, a TPA does *not* assume risk in the way that an insurer does. A number of states have adopted the NAIC Model Third-Party Administrator Act. *See* https://content.naic.org/sites/default/files/GL1090.pdf (last visited July 11, 2023).

States usually mandate that a TPA adhere to such requirements as:

- having a written contract with an insurer or self-funded health plan;
- keeping relevant records for at least five years, and being open to insurance department examinations and insurance company audits;
- receiving compensation that is *not* based on claims experience, i.e., not based on how many claims the TPA denies to make the experience more profitable, *but* compensation can be based on amount of premium collected and/or number of claims paid or processed;

---

[43]   *See, e.g.,* N.Y. Ins. L. § 2101(g).
[44]   *See, e.g.,* California Ins. Code § 14022; (exempting admitted attorneys and licensed insurance agents adjusting claims on business produced by them) and N.Y. Ins. L. § 2101(g) (allowing licensed property/casualty agents who receive no more than $50 to adjust claims to be exempt from obtaining a separate adjuster license).
[45]   *See, e.g.,* Texas Ins. Code § 4101.051 *et seq.*

- holding any premiums received in a separate fiduciary account;
- paying claims only with the authorization of the insurer or plan, and only from a separate claims-paying account;
- forwarding to insureds any policies, certificates, or other written communications from the insurance company; and
- sending a written notice to individual insureds explaining the relationship between the insurance company, the policyholder (e.g., the employer or union) and the TPA.[46]

E.   Reinsurance intermediaries

States license and regulate reinsurance intermediaries. A reinsurance intermediary negotiates and binds reinsurance for a direct ceding company which is buying reinsurance, or for an assuming reinsurer which is agreeing to reinsure the direct insurer. The NAIC has adopted a Reinsurance Intermediary Model Law for regulating reinsurance intermediaries.[47] All states have adopted the NAIC Model Law in an effort to effectively regulate reinsurance intermediaries, whose activities can materially affect the fiscal health of an insurer.[48]

Similar to the requirements imposed on MGAs, the laws require reinsurance intermediaries to agree to certain specified contract provisions such as, e.g., allowing the direct insurer on whose behalf the reinsurance intermediary is acting to terminate the contract for cause, the standards for cessions which the reinsurance intermediary must follow, the requirement that the reinsurance intermediary render timely accounts, and the requirement that the reinsurance intermediary retain certain specified records for at least ten years and submit to examinations by the insurer.

7.   Sanctions for Acting Without a Required License

State insurance regulators in the U.S. are authorized by statute to sanction unlicensed activities by both insurers and insurance professionals. State insurance codes permit state insurance departments to enforce licensing requirements by various means, including issuing administrative "cease

---

[46] *See, e.g.,* Ariz. Rev. Stat. §§ 20-485 *et seq.;* Iowa Ins. Code §§ 510.11 *et seq.*
[47] https://content.naic.org/sites/default/files/inline-files/MDL-790.pdf   (last visited July 11, 2023).
[48] *See, e.g.,* N.Y. Ins. L. § 2106; New Mexico Ins. Code Ch. 59A, Article 12D; Mass. G.L. ch.175, §§ 177 O *et seq.*

and desist" orders after providing the requisite notice of charges and affording the respondent a hearing. State insurance codes also authorize regulators to impose monetary penalties, and to seek court injunctions prohibiting illegal conduct. For example, in New York a person who acts as an insurance agent, broker or adjuster without the requisite license (or who is not exempt from licensure) can be subjected to a monetary penalty of $500 ($5,000 for illegally acting as an unlicensed reinsurance intermediary) for each illegal "transaction", which the New York State Department of Financial Services has interpreted to mean each insurance policy which the agent illegally placed or the unlicensed person illegally adjusted.[49]

Similarly, each person or entity who or which acts as an insurance company without being licensed can be penalized by an insurance department with administrative cease-and-desist orders, judicial injunctions and/or monetary penalties, and some states even make such unlicensed activity a crime.[50]

8.   Surplus Line or Excess Line Placements

As the major exception to their respective licensing requirements, states allow unlicensed—also called "non-admitted"—property and casualty insurers to operate under certain specified conditions in the "surplus line" or "excess line" markets. To legally insure a risk in a state in which the insurer is not admitted, the insurer must deal with a specially licensed broker called a "surplus line broker" or "excess line broker". That broker usually must first determine that a specified number of licensed insurers would decline to underwrite the risk at all or would only underwrite a portion of the risk.[51]

Alternatively, when the risk is one which licensed insurers are known to be generally unavailable to write, the risk can be written by non-admitted insurers without the surplus line or excess line broker having to first receive declinations from a certain number of admitted

---

[49]   N.Y. Ins. L. § 2102.
[50]   *See, e.g.,* Pennsylvania Statutes Title 40 P.S. Insurance § 626.12. (allows for fine of up to $5,000 per violation); RCW § 48.15.023 (in State of Washington unlicensed transaction of insurance can result in conviction of a Class B felony *and* up to $25,000 fine per violation).
[51]   *See, e.g.,* N.Y. Ins. L. § 2118.

insurers. These risks are specified on what are called "export lists". Insurance for amusement park rides is an example of such a risk.[52]

Surplus line or excess line insurance is NEVER permitted for ordinary personal lines coverages such as private passenger auto insurance or homeowner's insurance or life insurance, or health insurance, or annuities. Moreover, no surplus line insurer may write workers compensation insurance required by state law.

In the 2010 Dodd-Frank Act, to eliminate confusion by brokers, commercial policyholders, and state regulators, Congress specifically legislated that, in general, the state in which the policyholder is resident or has its principal place of business—known as the "home state"—will regulate the transaction, even if the policy covers multi-state risks.[53] Congress also sought to mandate uniformity as to which non-admitted insurers were eligible to be selected by the surplus line broker. For U.S. insurers which are non-admitted in the "home state", the insurer must be licensed in its domiciliary state to write the same kind of insurance AND have at least $15 million in capital and surplus *or* the minimum amount of capital and surplus required under the laws of the "home state", *whichever is greater*. (The "home state" regulator can lower the minimum capital surplus requirement to $4.5 million based on quality of the insurer's management, financial condition of parent company, availability of that kind of insurance in the marketplace, and any other relevant factor.)

For non-U.S. insurers, the "home state" must allow the surplus line broker to place the insurance with an insurer listed as approved on the NAIC International Insurers Department Quarterly Listing of Alien Insurers. The NAIC staff considers the insurer's financial condition, the amount of its capital and surplus, the quality of the regulatory apparatus in the country in which it is domiciled, the insurer's track record in paying claims, and other relevant factors before placing the insurer on the Quarterly Listing.

Under state surplus line regulations—which apply when the state is the "home state"—the surplus line broker is required to (i) obtain the requisite number of declinations from admitted insurers or, alternatively, confirm that the kind of insurance is on the "export list" and thus exempt

---

[52] *See, e.g.,* https://www.dfs.ny.gov/apps_and_licensing/property_insurers/current_export_list (last visited July 11, 2023).

[53] 15 U.S.C. 8202 *et seq.*

from the declination rules, and (ii) assess the solvency of the particular non-admitted insurer to be selected before placing the risk.[54]

The surplus line broker is also required to disclose in writing to the prospective policyholder that the insurance is being underwritten by an unlicensed company, that the state insurance department has not approved the rates or policy terms, and that the state property/casualty guaranty fund—which pays all or part of valid claims against insolvent insurers—will not cover this insurance. (New Jersey's guaranty fund does cover such claims for non-admitted medical malpractice insurers and property insurers covering small owner-occupied units.[55])

When the surplus line broker is placing insurance for a large commercial policyholder with numerous employees, and the policyholder has a professional risk manager with sufficiently large revenue and assets to be considered a sophisticated purchaser, the broker does not have to obtain the otherwise applicable number of declinations from admitted insurers. In the Dodd-Frank Act such a policyholder is called an "exempt commercial purchaser", and in some states this type of knowledgeable, large policyholder is termed an "industrial insured". Both the Dodd-Frank Act and various state "industrial insured" rules specify the conditions which the broker must meet to take advantage of this exemption. If a state does not have its own "industrial insured" exemption, a broker may use the exemption for "exempt commercial purchasers" set forth in the Dodd-Frank Act, *provided* the statutorily mandated conditions of minimum revenue, assets, and number of employees, are met.[56]

The surplus line broker must also disclose to the insured that coverage from licensed insurers is subject to greater regulation and, outside of New Jersey, the coverage is not eligible for state insurance guaranty fund protection. The policyholder must request in writing that coverage be placed with a non-admitted insurer.

---

[54] *See, e.g.,* 11 N.Y.C.R.R. Part 27 (N.Y. Dept. Financial Services Reg. 41).
[55] *See* N.J.S.A. § 17:22-6.70 *et seq.*
[56] *See* 15 U.S.C. § 8206(5); and *see, e.g.,* Ohio Rev. Code §3905.331.

5. How states monitor the financial condition of licensed insurance companies

All states utilize a panoply of laws, regulations, and procedures to monitor and supervise the financial condition of admitted, i.e. licensed, insurers. In this chapter we will discuss the principal regulatory tools.

I. REQUIRED FILINGS OF LICENSED INSURERS

Every U.S. state requires admitted insurance companies to file *quarterly and annual financial statements*, sworn to as accurate under penalty of perjury, using "statutory accounting principles" (SAP). These are more conservative than GAAP accounting rules. For example, under SAP, goodwill is not permitted to be accounted for as an asset of the insurer, no matter how longstanding and well-established the insurer's brand may be. SAP is premised on the supposition that the insurer is no longer an operating business. SAP supposes, hypothetically, that the insurer has stopped collecting premiums, and it measures how much the insurer has in assets, as of the statement date, to pay valid claims in full, allocated loss adjustment expenses, and unallocated loss adjustment expenses such as salaries, advertising, producer commissions, rent or debt service, taxes, interest, depreciation, and all other expenses. The NAIC has prepared this short but useful explanation of the differences between SAP and GAAP.[1]

States require quarterly financial statements on May 15 for the quarter ending March 31, August 15 for the quarter ending June 30, and November 15 for the quarter ending September 30. Each statement compares the current quarter with the results on the previous year's quarterly

---

[1] https://content.naic.org/cipr-topics/statutory-accounting-principles (last visited July 11, 2023).

statement for that quarter for each entry. For example, the first quarter 2024 statement due on May 15, 2024 will show the amount of premiums collected by the company in each state in which it does business by line of insurance and will also show the first quarter 2023 amount. Similarly, the statement will show the amount of losses paid in the first quarter of 2024 as compared with the first quarter of 2023.

Annual financial statements for the year ending the prior December 31 are due on March 1. Every licensed insurer must therefore file its 2023 Annual Financial Statement by March 1, 2024. Annual and quarterly statements historically were printed with blue covers for life and health insurers and with yellow covers for property and casualty insurers. You may hear someone refer to the "yellow book" or the "blue book" when discussing an insurer's financial statements. Today insurers file their financial statements through the NAIC electronic portal.

Besides showing premiums, losses and expenses, and various reserves, the financial statements also show the value of the insurer's investments in stocks, bonds, real estate, mortgages, swaps and collars and other derivatives, and all other investments, as well as the value of the reinsurance which the insurer has ceded and assumed, including any reinsurance recoveries that are in default. States expect strict compliance with the filing deadlines for financial statements. A series of interrogatories must also be answered. Failure to timely file can result in daily and cumulative penalties.[2]

There are numerous other filings which all U.S. states require of licensed insurers. The NAIC has prepared a comprehensive list of all required filings, including the financial statements. For example, the Utah Insurance Department has reproduced the list of required filings for all licensed life, accident, and health insurers, at: https://insurance.utah .gov/wp-content/uploads/ChecklistLifeAccidentHealthFraternal.pdf (last visited July 11, 2023).

For property and casualty insurers, the list is accessible at: https:// insurance.utah.gov/wp-content/uploads/ChecklistPropertyCasualty.pdf (last visited July 11, 2023).

---

[2]   *See, e.g.,* N.Y. Ins. L. § 307 (imposing penalty of $250 for each day of non-compliance up to a maximum aggregate of $25,000, in addition to license revocation or suspension, or initiation of liquidation or rehabilitation proceedings); N.J.S.A. Tit. 17 § 23-2 (daily penalty of $100 plus authority to do business can be suspended on notice to company).

For health insurers, the list is accessible at: https://insurance.utah.gov/ wp-content/uploads/ChecklistHealth.pdf (last visited July 11, 2023).

Of course, state insurance regulators often require specific state supplements, in addition to the NAIC forms which are mandated.[3]

In addition to quarterly and annual financial statements, and any applicable state supplements, admitted insurance companies must file a yearly *certification of the insurer's loss reserves* by a qualified actuary.[4] Another required filing is the annual *audit report by an independent certified public accountant* with disclosure to the insurer's board of directors of any material deficiencies in internal accounting.[5] (Insurers whose parent companies comply with similar provisions in the federal Sarbanes-Oxley Act for audits of their subsidiaries are not required to have separate audits.). Still other required annual filings include the submission to the insurer's domestic state insurance department of an *Own Risk Solvency Assessment* which identifies the material risks faced by the insurer and the processes by which the insurer addresses those risks, although insurers with less than $500 million in annual direct and assumed reinsurance premium are typically exempt.[6]

The 2008–09 financial crisis involved certain well-known insurance companies potentially having to pay out billions of dollars to credit default swap parties because an affiliate of those insurers, too lightly regulated by the federal Office of Thrift Supervision (a unit of the U.S. Treasury Department at the time) used the securities owned by those insurers as collateral for its own obligations. Fortunately, none of those insurers became insolvent, thanks to the herculean efforts of state insurance regulators working around the clock to unwind the contracts.

As a result of that experience, states now require the *parent company of most licensed insurers* to annually file an *Enterprise Risk Management Report* which, like the Management Discussion and Analysis section of a Form 10-K filed with the U.S. Securities & Exchange Commission, discusses material risks to the parent, affiliates and subsidiaries, how those risks affect the solvency of the insurer, and what the parent company, the

---

[3]   *See, e.g.,* https://www.dfs.ny.gov/apps_and_licensing/insurance _companies/annual_statements_ny_supplements (last visited July 11, 2023) (links to various supplements which the N.Y. Dept. of Fin. Serv. requires New York-licensed insurers to file).

[4]   *See, e.g.,* Title 24-A: Maine Insurance Code § 993.

[5]   *See, e.g.,* Ohio Administrative Code § 3901-1-50.

[6]   *See, e.g.,* Va. Code § 38.2-1334.3 *et seq.*

insurer and subsidiaries and affiliates are doing to address and manage those risks. A company which discusses the same topics in its annual 10-K Statement filed with the SEC may file a copy of that Statement, in lieu of the Enterprise Risk Management Report, but the copy filed with the state insurance regulator must be marked to show that the required topics are, in fact, discussed.[7]

Besides requiring parent companies to submit annual Enterprise Risk Management Reports, state insurance regulators have the power to obtain information about the parent company and the insurer's affiliates by requiring the insurer to produce whatever relevant information it can lawfully obtain about the parent and affiliates.[8]

One other result of the 2008–09 financial crisis was the concern on the part of state insurance regulators that licensed insurers needed to be more transparent as to their policies and procedures for making corporate decisions and allocating power and responsibility within the companies. In 2014 the NAIC issued the Corporate Governance Annual Disclosure Model Act and associated Model Regulations, requiring annual filing of a Corporate Governance Annual Disclosure In the words of the NAIC summary, the annual filing must disclose:

> confidential information about their corporate governance framework. This includes the policies of their boards of directors and key committees, the frequency of their meetings, and the procedure for the oversight of critical risk areas and appointment practices…[and] the policies and practices used by their board of directors for directing senior management on critical areas. This includes a description of codes of business conduct and ethics and processes for performance evaluation, compensation practices, corrective action, succession planning, and suitability standards.[9]

The deadline for filing is typically June 1 of each year. The Annual Disclosure must be signed and certified by the CEO or Secretary of the insurer. To avoid duplicating previous filings, if appropriate, insurers are allowed to state that no material changes have been effected since the last filing.

A very important required annual filing is the set of *Risk based capital (RBC) calculations* which most insurers must perform and submit to the

---

[7] *See, e.g.,* Tex. Admin Code Rule §7.214.
[8] *See, e.g.,* Md. Ins. Code § 7-605.
[9] https://content.naic.org/cipr-topics/corporate-governance (last visited July 11, 2023).

domestic regulator (and to any ancillary regulator if requested) using a very complicated formula developed by the NAIC and legislated by states. The RBC Report measures how much capital the insurer needs to adequately deal with various risks, such as (i) underwriting risk—how frequent and severe its losses will be and the amount of allocated loss adjustment expenses projected, (ii) asset risk—how likely that its investments will decline in value and by how much—and (iii) credit risk—how likely will persons and entities which are indebted to the insurer will default on their respective obligations and by how much.[10]

Risk based capital calculations were first used by banking regulators in Europe, but by the early 1990s U.S. insurance regulators had begun to require licensed insurers to submit them annually. The NAIC developed and periodically updates the various formulae for calculating an insurer's risk based capital, depending on whether the company is a life insurer, a property-casualty insurer, or a health insurer. All states have adopted RBC laws. The NAIC has prepared a helpful explanation of the RBC process: https://content.naic.org/cipr-topics/risk-based-capital (last visited July 11, 2023).

RBC reports are confidential and not subject to public disclosure, lest an ominous RBC Report spark policyholders to cancel and lapse policies without justification. Nor may any insurer or producer use an RBC report in advertising in order to prevent consumer confusion and deception.[11]

State laws mandating RBC calculations provide for varying levels of regulatory action depending on how deficient an insurer's RBC level is when calculated. An insurer with an RBC level slightly below the level which the regulator considers optimal according to a statutory formula, is required to file a "Company Action Plan", for review and approval, indicating how the insurer intends to correct the deficiency.[12] An insurer whose RBC level is considerably below that which its domestic regulator considers optimal, or whose "Company Action Plan" has failed to achieve its objectives, is likely to receive a "Regulatory Action Plan" in which the regulator prescribes certain requirements which the insurer must fulfill.[13] Insurers subject to such plans and directives may be also

---

[10] *See, e.g.,* Title XXXVII N.H. Rev. Stat. Chapter 404-F.
[11] *See, e.g.,* N.H. Rev. Stat. 404-F:8.
[12] *See, e.g.,* N.H. Rev. Stat. § 404-F:3.
[13] *See, e.g.,* N.H. Rev. Stat. § 404-F:4.

placed into confidential "administrative supervision" which is discussed in detail in Chapter 6.

II.   PERIODIC ON-SITE EXAMINATIONS

Another set of U.S. state laws require periodic on-site examinations conducted by state insurance department examiners, or by examiners under contract to the department, usually every three years, but sometimes more frequently at the absolute discretion of the regulators. These examinations are typically done by the insurer's state of domicile, but any state that licenses the insurer has the power to examine it *at any time*.[14] Insurers must pay the cost of these examinations.

The examination starts with interviews by the examiners of key executives and an examination scope letter from the examiners to the company describing the scope of the examination and the particular company records the examiners want to see. *If you are advising the insurer, you need to make sure the insurer can promptly produce requested documents to the examiners and make available knowledgeable company officials for questioning.*

Lawyers need to know how the law of the examining state treats documents that qualify for the attorney-client privilege or attorney work-product privilege in case the examiners demand to see them. In some states the production of documents demanded by department examiners will *not* be treated as a voluntary waiver of the privilege, so that the company does not lose the protection if a third party, such as a civil court plaintiff, seeks to discover them, assuming the document otherwise qualifies for the privilege and the insurer initially refuses to provide the document(s) on the basis of the privilege or privileges.[15] In other states, however, even if the production is mandatory under insurance regulatory laws, the company voluntarily producing the document to department examiners will often constitute a waiver, although courts are reluctant

---

[14]   *See, e.g.,* Tex. Ins. Code §§ 401.051, 401.052.
[15]   *See, e.g., Diversified Indus., Inc. v. Meredith,* 572 F.2d 596, 606 (8th Cir. 1977) (en banc); *see also Teachers Insurance and Annuity Assn. v. Shamrock Broadcasting Co., Inc.,* 521 F. Supp. 638 (S.D.N.Y. 1981) (discussing decisions reaching opposite results and ordering hearing to determine which particular documents in that case qualified for invocation of the privilege).

to adopt rigid all-encompassing rules, instead preferring to rule on a case-by-case basis after analyzing the factual setting.[16]

BOX 5.1   PRACTICAL TIPS FOR PRACTITIONERS

If examiners demand documents from your client or your company, which otherwise qualify for privileged status, and the U.S. state law is uncertain as to whether the privilege would be waived if the documents were produced, consider the following alternatives:

Instead of producing the documents, offer to produce all relevant non-privileged documents *and* to make available all knowledgeable company officials who will describe all of the relevant facts for the examiners and answer questions, but will not recount what questions they posed to company attorneys or what legal advice they received.

If this is not acceptable to the examiners, request the examiners to put their demand for the privileged documents in writing with a citation to the statute or regulation requiring the company to produce the documents for examination *and* request that the examiners state in writing that the insurance department will not deem the production to be a voluntary waiver. The examiners' statement is not binding on any U.S. court adjudicating a subsequent third-party action, but it could bolster an argument to the court that the mandatory production to the examiners did not effect a voluntary waiver by the insurance company if the applicable law on the point is uncertain.

Examination reports on insurance companies are public documents once they have been finally approved. States allow insurers the opportunity to see and comment, and even have a formal hearing in some states, on draft examination reports before final adoption.[17] The information, records and workpapers compiled by examiners are exempt from public disclosure.[18]

---

[16]   *See, e.g., In re Steinhardt Partners*, 9 F.3d 230 (2d Cir. 1993).
[17]   *See, e.g.,* N.Y. Ins. L. § 311.
[18]   *See, e.g.,* Michigan Ins. Code § 500.222.

III.   REGULATION OF INSURANCE COMPANY INVESTMENTS

States regulate investments by licensed insurers, specifying in detail what types of investments are permissible—e.g., U.S. Treasury bills, bank certificates of deposit, common stocks, preferred stocks, real estate, mortgages, foreign government and foreign company investments—and what is the maximum percentage of assets that can be invested in a particular type of investment. State insurance regulators permit investment in various forms of derivatives, but many states require the insurer to submit, and receive regulatory approval for, a detailed "derivative use plan".[19]

Insurance departments allow insurers to devote a relatively small percentage of assets in investments that are not expressly permitted. These are called "basket" or "leeway" investments.[20] An insurer that makes an impermissible investment which is neither expressly allowed nor permitted as a "basket" investment will have the value of the impermissible investment deducted from its "admitted assets" when examined by the relevant state insurance department.[21]

Although in recent years Congress has limited the power of ancillary state regulators to supervise transactions, such as reinsurance, involving insurers which are licensed in those states but not domiciled there, Congress has not yet limited the power of ancillary states to regulate the investments of licensed insurance companies—even if they are not domestic insurers. New York has been the most aggressive in regulating the investments of all licensed insurers, even if they are not domiciled in New York, and requiring them to substantially comply with investment rules that New York domestic insurers must follow, absent specific regulatory approval for non-compliant investments.[22] Other states require their domestic insurers to follow investment restrictions, but do not attempt to impose their investment rules on licensed insurance companies domiciled elsewhere.

---

[19]   *See, e.g.,* N.Y. Ins. L. § 1410.
[20]   *See, e.g.,* N.Y. Ins. L. § 1405(a)(8) for life insurers prescribing various percentage limitations depending on the type of investment.
[21]   *See, e.g.,* N.Y. Ins. L. § 1412.
[22]   See N.Y. Ins. L. § 1413.

IV. REGULATION OF REINSURANCE ARRANGEMENTS OF DOMESTIC INSURERS

States regulate how admitted insurers account for reinsurance which they purchase. Licensed insurers may buy reinsurance from licensed or "accredited" or "certified" reinsurers and receive full credit for the reinsurance on their required quarterly or annual financial statements as a deduction of their liabilities or an increase in assets. If a reinsurer is in default for 90 days or more, and the default is not in dispute, the licensed company is not allowed to take full credit for the amount of unpaid reinsurance on its financial statements.

Licensed insurers may buy reinsurance from unlicensed reinsurers, but they are *not* usually allowed to take credit for the reinsurance on their financial statements *unless* the reinsurer, especially those reinsurers domiciled outside of the U.K. and EU, has collateralized the liabilities it will owe to the licensed company. Recent international agreements negotiated by the Federal Insurance Office and the U.S. Trade Representative have modified this requirement for certain EU and U.K. reinsurers who meet a specified level of capital, and who enjoy among the highest claims-paying ratings from reputable rating services. All states have ceased enforcing collateral requirements on reinsurers domiciled in the U.K. and EU nations which meet the criteria for exemption set forth in the respective "covered agreements". These "covered agreements" are discussed in Chapter 2 at pp. 24–25 and are detailed in Chapter 9 at pp. 119–121.

For reinsurers who do not qualify for exemption under the U.K. and EU "covered agreements" the collateral which states require to secure the liabilities those reinsurers owe to the licensed ceding insurers must take three basic forms:

(1)   a trust set up by the reinsurer in a U.S. licensed financial institution covering the projected liabilities (often known as a "Reg. 114 trust" after Regulation 114 of the N.Y. Dept. of Financial Services) and which the licensed insurer can access without needing the reinsurer's consent; or

(2)   an irrevocable letter of credit from a U.S. licensed financial institution covering the amount of the liabilities, which does not need the reinsurer's consent for the licensed insurer to draw upon; or

(3)   a "funds withheld" arrangement by which the licensed insurer withholds the amount of the projected liabilities from the reinsur-

ance premium that would otherwise be paid to the reinsurer, and if the amount of liabilities exceeds the amount withheld, then the reinsurer must pay the balance to the ceding insurer within a time specified in the reinsurance contract.[23]

When a state insurance department conducts an on-site examination of a licensed insurance company, the examiners routinely audit the reinsurance arrangements the company has with unlicensed reinsurers. The examiners thoroughly check to see if the unlicensed reinsurer, not covered by the FIO agreements with the U.K. and EU, has posted acceptable collateral in the form of a suitable trust or letter of credit, or if the reinsurance contract includes a permissible "funds withheld" provision.

States also require that the licensed insurer include a clause in every reinsurance contract under which the reinsurer agrees to pay the liquidator of the licensed company, if liquidation proceedings occur, "without diminution". This means that a reinsurer cannot argue that the liquidator is not entitled to recover any amount under the reinsurance contract because the liquidator has not yet paid policyholders and claimants the full amount of direct insurance under the reinsured policies originally issued by the liquidated insurance company.[24]

Before 2011 states could regulate the reinsurance transactions of any licensed insurer, even if it were domiciled in another state. For example, New York regulators required all licensed companies which wanted to claim credit on their financial statements filed with New York by having an unlicensed reinsurer set up a "Reg. 114 trust", to only deal with reinsurers willing to have the trust assets invested according to New York's strict investment laws. As another example, California invoked Cal. Ins. Code § 1011(c) to require that all licensed companies, no matter whether they were domiciled in California or not, obtain California Insurance Department approval before ceding 75 percent or more of the risk to any reinsurer.

In Section 531 of the federal Dodd-Frank Act,[25] Congress explicitly preempted such ancillary state rules by enacting a provision making the *domestic state of the ceding insurer* the exclusive regulator of reinsurance transactions executed by that domestic ceding insurer on one condition:

---

[23] *See, e.g.,* Cal. Ins. Code § 922.4; 11 N.Y.C.R.R. Parts 125 and 126 and Code of West Virginia § 33-4-15a.
[24] *See, e.g.,* N.Y. Ins. L. § 1308.
[25] 15 U.S.C. § 8221 *et seq.*

the state must be an "accredited state" by the National Association of Insurance Commissioners or have financial solvency laws equivalent to NAIC-accredited states. Section 531 of the Dodd-Frank Act affecting reinsurance transactions is the one Congressional enactment which expressly applies the NAIC accreditation standards and incorporates them into federal law. You will recall that another provision of the Dodd-Frank Act, 15 U.S.C. § 8202, applies an NAIC Model Law on surplus line insurance and the NAIC list of non-U.S. surplus line insurers, but that section—making the "home state" of the policyholder the exclusive regulator of surplus line insurance transactions by the policyholder—does not incorporate the NAIC accreditation standards.

The credit for reinsurance rules enforced by state insurance regulators on unlicensed companies apply to "indemnity reinsurance" in which the licensed direct insurer receives indemnity, i.e., reimbursement, according to the terms of the reinsurance contract with the unlicensed reinsurer, but the direct insurer remains liable to policyholders and claimants on the direct policies reinsured under the reinsurance contract. It is a fundamental principle of reinsurance law that ordinarily a policyholder or claimant under a direct insurance policy has no claim against a reinsurer which has agreed only to indemnify the direct ceding insurer according to the terms of the reinsurance contract. Only if the policyholder or claimant can invoke a specific "cut-through" endorsement in the policy issued by the direct insurer can she or he claim against one or more of the reinsurers.[26]

Some states also regulate "assumption reinsurance" transactions under which the original licensed direct insurer transfers its obligations under a block of policies to an assuming reinsurer, also licensed in that state, which is substituted as the direct insurer on those particular policies. Assumption reinsurance transactions typically require regulatory approval, and in some states, the policyholders must consent either expressly or tacitly by making a specified number of premium payments to the substituted direct insurer without objecting to the transfer.[27]

---

[26]   *See, e.g.,* NAIC Task Force on Reinsurance, White Paper on Reinsurance Collateral, 2006, p. 4   accessible at https://content.naic.org/sites/default/files/inline-files/cmte_e_reinsurance_related_2016_whitepaper.pdf (last visited July 11, 2023); *see also Squibb-Mathieson Int'l Corp. v. St. Paul Mercury Ins. Co.,* 44 Misc. 2d. 835 (N.Y. Sup. Ct. 1964) and cases cited therein.

[27]   *See, e.g.,* N.C. Gen. Stat. §§ 58-10-20 to 58-10-45; Ore. Rev. Stat. §§ 742.150 to 742.162.

V. REQUIRING INSURERS TO DETECT AND REPORT SUSPECTED FRAUDULENT CLAIMS

U.S. state insurance departments typically require all licensed insurers to establish and maintain robust and detailed policies and procedures to detect and report fraudulent claims that, if paid, would be detrimental to the insurer's financial condition. States have issued stringent regulations mandating that insurance companies hire, train, and deploy investigators, lawyers, forensic accountants, and other staff to perform this critical function, and to set up both consistent internal reporting procedures when claims personnel suspect fraud, and external reporting procedures when reporting to insurance regulators and law enforcement is warranted. Often, insurance companies will utilize former law enforcement personnel with deep expertise in detecting suspected fraud. Insurers must adhere to detailed anti-fraud plans that must be submitted for regulatory approval.[28]

VI. REQUIRING COMPLIANCE WITH CYBERSECURITY STANDARDS

Just within the past several years U.S. state insurance regulators have begun to require compliance with detailed cybersecurity rules, partly as a financial solvency measure to minimize the risk that insurers would need to spend millions of dollars, for which they had collected no premiums, in reimbursing policyholders and claimants for damages and other costs of remedying massive data breaches. Another motivation was to ensure that insurers and agents engage in proper market conduct, discussed in detail in Chapter 7, to safeguard personal, non-public information given to them by policyholders and claimants.

New York became the first state in 2017 to issue stringent cybersecurity regulations which all licensed insurers, agents, brokers, and all other licensed persons must follow—unless they have a limited exemption as a "small business", or are a captive insurer, certified or accredited reinsurer, or risk retention group domiciled outside of New York. 11

---

[28] *See, e.g.,* N.J.A.C. 11:16-6; N.Y. Ins. L. Article 4; *see also* https://www.insurance.ca.gov/0400-news/0100-press-releases/2023/release006-2023.cfm (last visited July 11, 2023).

N.Y.C.R.R. Part 500 sets forth the various requirements imposed on all licensees, including agents and brokers, unless the licensee qualifies for exemption from some, but not all, of the requirements as a "small business". Among the cybersecurity requirements imposed by the New York Department of Financial Services (DFS) are: a mandatory risk assessment to measure how vulnerable the company is to a data breach, the appointment of, and reporting by, a Chief Information Security Officer, various required penetration testing measures, multi-factor authentication, regular cybersecurity awareness training of all employees, a detailed written plan for responding to, and reporting, data breaches, requirements for third-party service contractors, and an annual certification filed with the DFS that the company is in full compliance with the regulation.[29] In 2022 the DFS announced it was proposing to make the regulations in Part 500 even more stringent.[30]

The NAIC has issued a Model Act on Insurer Data Security which largely follows the original New York DFS regulation. https://www.naic.org/store/free/MDL-668.pdf (last visited July 11, 2023). South Carolina adopted the NAIC Model Law as part of its Insurance Code in 2018.[31] Ohio, Indiana, Michigan and Mississippi are among other states which more recently enacted similar regulations. Unlike the New York DFS regulation, the other state laws do not require filings of annual certifications of compliance from all licensed insurance professionals and all foreign and alien insurers. Instead, those laws require annual certifications be filed only by *domestic* insurance companies.[32]

VII.   THE INSURER HOLDING COMPANY ACTS

One of the most important solvency regulation tools used by U.S. state insurance regulators is their respective state laws colloquially called the "Holding Company Acts". Every state has enacted a very similar version of the NAIC Model Insurer Holding Company System Act, authorizing that state's insurance regulators to monitor and prohibit (i) excessive dividends from the insurer to its parent company that could be detrimental

---

[29]   https://www.dfs.ny.gov/legal/regulations/adoptions/dfsrf500txt.pdf   (last visited July 11, 2023).

[30]   https://www.dfs.ny.gov/industry_guidance/cybersecurity (last visited July 11, 2023).

[31]   S.C. Ins. Code § 38-99-10.

[32]   *See, e.g.,* S.C. Ins. Code § 38-99-20 (I); Ala. Code § 27-62-4.

to the insurer's solvency and (ii) transactions between the insurer and its parent and/or affiliates, such as, e.g., service agreements or reinsurance agreements, which are unreasonably favorable to the non-insurer party or parties. An example of this would be a service agreement between the insurer and parent company which provides for the employees of the parent company to perform services for the insurer, such as IT operations, but also requiring the insurer to pay excessive fees to its parent for those services.[33] Another feature of state versions of the Holding Company Act is regulation of who can acquire control over an insurance company operating in the state.

Beginning in 1969 when New York adopted the first Holding Company Act, now codified as Article 15 of the New York Insurance Law, the state versions applied only to domestic insurers, not those domiciled elsewhere but admitted in a state. During the 1990s some states expanded the scope of their respective Holding Company Acts to cover "commercially domiciled" insurers which wrote a significant, statutorily specified, proportion of their business in those states that exceeded the amount of premium which the insurer wrote in their domestic state in the last calendar year.

States like New York and California deem these insurers to be "commercially domiciled" and subject to their respective insurer holding company acts, so anyone who or which wants to acquire 10 percent of more of their shares (or shares in a controlling company) must, unless regulators specifically waive the requirement, get approval in that state as well as the official domiciliary state.[34] Some states with "commercial domicile" provisions in their version of the Holding Company Act, like California, require insurers to obtain regulatory approval for inter-company transactions as if the insurer were officially domiciled in the state. Thus, insurance companies deemed "commercially domiciled" may need to obtain two sets of regulatory approvals, depending on the wording of the relevant state laws: approval from its official domicile and approval from the state in which it is deemed "commercially domiciled". California also requires every licensed company to obtain its approval before a merger with another insurance company under Section 1011(c) of the California Insurance Code.

---

[33]   *See, e.g.,* Mass. G.L. ch. 175, § 206 *et seq.*; South Dakota Ins. Code § 58-5A-1 *et seq.*

[34]   *See, e.g.,* Cal. Ins. Code § 1215.14; N.Y. Ins. L. § 1501(d) (life insurers).

BOX 5.2   PRACTICAL TIP FOR PRACTITIONERS

Always determine if any insurer involved in your legal analysis is deemed, or could potentially be deemed, to be "commercially domiciled" in a state, other than its official domicile, for purposes of complying with the version of the Holding Company Act in that ancillary state.

The principal insurance regulatory objectives of state insurer Holding Company Acts are:

1.   Prohibiting Excessive Dividends

The main purpose of a state insurer Holding Company System Act is to prevent parent companies from unfairly and unreasonably using the assets of the licensed insurer to the detriment of policyholders, claimants, other creditors, and the public. Under each state's version of the Holding Company Act, domestic insurers must obtain express approval in advance for dividends paid by insurers to parent companies, *if* the proposed dividend is considered "extraordinary".[35]

It is critical to know how a particular state defines the term "extraordinary dividend". Some states, like Arizona and Mississippi, define that term in such a way as to require advance approval if a domestic insurer wants to pay a dividend of more than the LESSER of either 10 percent of surplus *or* the amount of last year's net income (or net gain from operations if a life insurer) calculated using the last filed Annual Statement. *This formula makes it more likely that advance regulatory approval will be required*, and most states require 30 days' advance notice of the insurer's intention to pay an "extraordinary dividend".[36]

In other states, however, the definition allows insurers to pay more dividends without advance regulatory approval. In these states an "extraordinary dividend" is one in which the amount of the dividend from the domestic insurer exceeds the GREATER of 10 percent of surplus *or* the amount of last year's net income (or net gain from operations if a life insurer). *Under this formula the need to obtain advance regulatory*

---

[35]   *See, e.g.,* Conn. G.S. § 38a-136.
[36]   *See, e.g.,* Ariz. Rev. Stat. § 20-481.19; Miss. Code § 83-6-25 (45 day advance notice required)).

approval will be less frequent than in states with the phrase "lesser of" *in their definitions of* "extraordinary dividend".[37]

2.   Regulating Transactions Between the Insurer and its Parent and/or its Affiliates

Every insurer that is a subsidiary of a parent company must file, and keep current, a *Form B Registration Statement* with its domestic state, to which all ancillary states have access. This filing shows the insurance company's relationship to the parent company, e.g., what percentage of its stock is owned by controlling persons, and its relationship to sister companies. Information as to the identity of the insurer's and controlling entity's officers and directors must be disclosed, along with a description of material transactions between the insurer and parent and/or affiliates.[38]

States have legislated several basic rules governing transactions between the insurer and its parent and/or affiliates, again to prevent the insurer's assets from being unfairly depleted. States require that:

(1)   the terms of the inter-company transaction shall be fair and reasonable;

(2)   charges or fees for services performed shall be reasonable;

(3)   expenses incurred and payment received shall be allocated to the insurer in conformity with customary insurance accounting practices consistently applied;

(4)   the books, accounts and records of each party to all such transactions shall be so maintained as to clearly and accurately disclose the nature and details of the transactions including such accounting information as is necessary to support the reasonableness of the charges or fees to the respective parties; and

(5)   the insurer's surplus as regards policyholders following any dividends or distributions to shareholder affiliates shall be reasonable in relation to the insurer's outstanding liabilities and adequate to its financial needs.[39]

---

[37]   *See, e.g.,* Mass. G.L. ch. 175, § 206C; Tex. Ins. Code § 823.107; Mich. Ins. Code § 500.1343..

[38]   *See, e.g.,* Mass. G.L. ch. 175, § 206C.

[39]   *See, e.g.,* Mass. G.L. ch. 175, § 206C; Georgia Code § 33-13-5.

Management or service contracts and tax allocation agreements, e.g., between an insurer and its parent, or between or among an insurer and its affiliate(s), which exceed a certain specified percentage of the insurer's assets or surplus must be submitted for approval in advance to domestic regulator or commercial domestic regulator, as do reinsurance agreements depending on the amount of reinsurance. The insurer will file a *Form D* with its domestic regulator (and with the insurance department of a state in which it is deemed "commercially domiciled" if the law of that state so requires) explaining the reason(s) for the transaction, summarizing its terms and conditions, and attaching a copy of the proposed inter-company agreement.

Depending on the state's insurance laws, any loans, transfers, or guarantees made by an insurer that in value equal or exceed a statutorily specified percentage of the insurer's assets or surplus must also be either noticed to the regulator in advance or receive actual approval in advance.[40]

3. Requiring the Enterprise Risk Management Report, or the Management Discussion and Analysis Section of the Filed SEC 10-K Statement, to be Filed by the Insurer's Parent Company

As discussed above, in recent years states have amended their respective Holding Company Acts to require parent companies to file a *Form F* Enterprise Risk Statement discussing risks to the parent, the insurer, and affiliates and how the various entities are dealing with such risks. Holding companies which file a 10-K Annual Statement with the SEC may file a copy of the Management Discussion and Analysis part of that Statement *provided* it discusses the same topics which the state regulation requires be discussed in a Form F.

---

[40] *See, e.g.*, N.Y. Ins. L. § 1505 (requiring actual approval for some transactions); Kansas Ins. Code § 40-3306 (providing for deemed approval after 30 days if regulator asserts no objection).

4.   Requiring that Information Compiled in Administering the Holding Company Act by the State Insurance Department (or Equivalent Agency) Ordinarily be Kept Confidential

Naturally, insurers and parent companies are very reluctant to have information filed pursuant to the requirements of a state Holding Company Act available to competitors or the general public. Therefore, many states have enacted provisions which require that the information be kept confidential, notwithstanding state freedom-of-information laws, unless the commissioner (or equivalent official) decides to release it "in the public interest" after notice to the insurer and due consideration of any objections by the company to the release.[41] State insurance regulators have allowed public release of such information in extremely rare circumstances, if ever.

5.   Regulating Who can Acquire Control Over a Domestic or "Commercially Domiciled" Insurance Company

Along with regulating transactions between and among a licensed insurer, its parent company, and any subsidiaries and/or affiliates, the other principal function of state insurer Holding Company Acts is to regulate who can take control of the licensed insurer. To some extent the procedures that state insurance departments use in so doing resemble those applicable to the primary and expansion UCAA licensing process, discussed in Chapter 4, with certain important modifications and additions.

The state insurer Holding Company Acts broadly define the term "control". "Control" means the power to direct or manage the insurer's affairs, *directly or indirectly*. So anyone that controls a company which, in turn, controls an insurer as a second-tier subsidiary is deemed to have acquired "control" over the insurer.[42] "Control" is presumed, by law, if a person owns or controls 10 percent or more of the voting shares of the insurer or of a company that owns or controls 10 percent or more of the voting shares of the insurer.

Regulators have discretion to exempt persons who have more than this 10 percent stake on a convincing showing that the person will be

---

[41]   *See, e.g.,* Nev. Rev. Stat. § 692C.420; South Carolina Ins. Code § 38-21-290.

[42]   *See, e.g.,* Mass. G.L. ch. 175, § 206.

a strictly "passive" investor, taking no part at all in the management of the insurer, and not voting her or his or its shares to elect Board members of the insurer or the company that controls the insurer. This is called a "disclaimer of control" and requires a detailed written application to the regulators.[43]

If an individual or entity seeks to acquire "control" of a domestic insurer, they must file with the insurer's domestic regulator (and the ancillary state regulator if the insurer is deemed "commercially domiciled" in that state) a detailed statement called a "Form A Statement" explaining the transaction by which they would acquire control. The Form A Statement must include a detailed description of the applicant's plans for the insurer, specific to the insurance marketplace in that state, and a set of *pro forma* financial projections showing projected premiums, losses, loss expenses and other expenses, and various reserves, as well as projected reinsurance to be bought and sold by the insurer.

An example of the Form A Statement required by the Nevada Division of Insurance, using a form developed by the NAIC appears at: http://doi.nv.gov/uploadedFiles/doinvgov/_public-documents/Insurers/form_a.pdf (last visited July 11, 2023).

Accompanying a Form A Statement must be biographical affidavits of all officers and directors of the insurer and any company that directly or indirectly controls the insurer. Regulators have discretion to limit who must submit these affidavits so that it is sometimes possible to avoid having the CEO of a huge company submit an affidavit when only the officers and directors of its fourth-tier insurance subsidiary, and the officers and directors of its third-tier intermediate holding company that would own all the insurer's shares, will have anything to do with managing the insurer. Some states may require fingerprints of each person who is required to submit a biographical affidavit.[44]

The affidavits are the same as those used to obtain an insurance company license, and include questions on the affiant's licenses, official investigations, and non-traffic criminal convictions, as well as any bankruptcy proceeding involving the affiant. Whatever information is set forth on any required biographical affidavit must be totally complete

---

[43] *See, e.g.,* New Mexico Ins. Code § 59A-37-19.
[44] *See, e.g.,* https://www.tdi.texas.gov/insurer/documents/clrfingerprint.pdf; https://www.floir.com/siteDocuments/Applications/AcquisitionControllingInterestFloridaDomesticInsurerLHPC.pdf (last visited July 11, 2023).

and accurate. States routinely retain third-party verification vendors, at the applicant's expense, to verify every single answer on the affidavit.[45] *No answer on the affidavit should be left blank for any reason.* If the information sought is not applicable to that particular affiant, the affiant should state: "NO" or "NONE" depending on the information sought.[46]

Regulators typically take between 90 and 180 days to review all the information in the Form A submission, including, the proposed business plan, biographical affidavits, verification reports, and financial projections. Depending on the degree of public interest that regulators perceive in the proposed acquisition, they may schedule a public hearing. At the hearing the applicant and insurer's executives will have to testify under oath and be subject to cross-examination.[47] Policyholders and consumer groups are permitted to submit statements, present testimony, and cross-examine. In some states parties who appear at the public hearing are allowed to demand pre-hearing discovery from the insurer and/or the applicant subject to supervision by the insurance department.[48]

In deciding whether to grant the application and approve the acquisition of control, the Holding Company Acts require that regulators basically consider whether after the acquisition the domestic insurer (and, where applicable, the "commercially domiciled" insurer) will be able to comply with all applicable laws and regulations, whether the proposed management of the insurer has the requisite competence, experience and integrity, and whether the acquisition would be detrimental to policyholders, creditors and the public. It is very rare for applications to be denied, but regulators routinely condition their approval on explicit conditions to which the applicant has committed to meeting in writing, such as agreeing not to seek dividends for a specified period of time.

Most of the time counsel for applicants spend in dealing with regulators on acquisitions is in meeting with them before and after the Form A Statement is filed and negotiating these conditions. An example of how U.S. state insurance regulators impose detailed conditions for approving applications for acquisition of control under state versions of the Holding Company Act appears in the New York State Department of Financial Service 2018 Order approving, conditionally, the acquisition by CVS

---

[45] *See, e.g.,* https://www.naic.org/industry_ucaa_biographical_report.htm (last visited July 11, 2023).

[46] https://content.naic.org/industry_ucaa_faq.htm (last visited July 11, 2023).

[47] *See, e.g.,* Mass. G.L. ch. 175, § 206B(d).

[48] *See, e.g.,* N.H. Rev. Stat. 401-B:3.

of the New York insurer owned by Aetna. *See* https://www.dfs.ny.gov/
reports_and_publications/press_releases/pr1811261 (last visited July 11,
2023).

In rare situations, a state which is not the official domicile or commercial domicile of the insurer being acquired can decide if the acquisition
would be anti-competitive in that state's insurance market. Where the
acquiring entity is itself an insurance company or controls an insurance
company that competes with the target insurer in the same line of insurance, and if the two insurance companies have a market share of at least 4
percent in the state for that line of insurance, or other statutorily specified
conditions apply, the acquiring entity must file a *Form E* with the state's
insurance regulators explaining why the acquisition would not unduly
lessen competition.[49] Applicants in these situations typically retain expert
economists as consultants to prepare a report, to be submitted to the
state's insurance regulators, which aims to minimize the anti-competitive
effect of the acquisition.

BOX 5.3   PRACTICAL TIP FOR PRACTITIONERS:

As of 2023, the NAIC had published color-coded maps of which U.S.
jurisdictions had adopted the latest version of the Insurer Holding
Company System Model Act and the associated Model Regulation.
https://content.naic.org/sites/default/files/inline-files/440%20GCC
%20LST%209.01.2022%20Final-combined.pdf (last visited July 11,
202).

---

6.   **Texas Regulates Who can Acquire Control Over an
        Insurance Agency**

Alone among state insurance departments, only the Texas Department
of Insurance requires anyone or any entity seeking to acquire control
over a licensed insurance agency, *whether resident or non-resident*, to
file information about the acquiror, including a biographical affidavit
for each individual by whom control will be exercised, and wait at least
60 days to see if the Department sends any objection to the acquisition.

---

[49]   *See, e.g.,* Indiana Code § 27-1-23-2.5.

The filing must be under the signature of a person already licensed as an insurance agent in Texas.[50]

---

[50] Texas Ins. Code § 4001.253.

6. How U.S. state insurance regulators deal with financially troubled insurance companies

When a U.S. insurer becomes financially impaired or insolvent, state insurance regulators utilize three basic types of proceedings:

I. CONFIDENTIAL ADMINISTRATIVE SUPERVISION

As discussed in Chapter 5, after performing the annually required Risk Based Capital (RBC) calculation, when an insurer has a significantly deficient RBC level as measured by the RBC formula, or if it has been downgraded severely by rating agencies and its financial condition is uncertain or threatened, regulators can impose "administrative supervision" in the form of a written "Order of Supervision". Such an order requires the insurer to obtain approval for essentially all important management decisions and imposes financial limits on the insurer's operations. Often the regulators will appoint a department official to work on-site at the insurer's headquarters to implement the Order of Supervision. The procedure is confidential in order to avoid inciting policyholders to cancel or surrender policies in large numbers in a way that would be destabilizing.

When a domestic regulator places an insurance company into "administrative supervision" the regulator will specify what actions will require advance approval, such as writing new business, paying claims over a specified amount, paying dividends to the parent company, or entering into reinsurance arrangements. This recent administrative supervision order from the Florida Office of Insurance Regulation, unusual in being public, is an example.[1]

---

[1] http://www.trbas.com/media/media/acrobat/2017-08/70148366491440 -29120635.pdf (last visited July 11, 2023).

II.   REHABILITATION (IN CALIFORNIA CONSERVATION)

An insurer whose RBC level is so deficient as to constitute a hazardous financial condition, whether or not actually insolvent, will be placed into rehabilitation or liquidation proceedings on the request of the domestic regulator made to the courts in that state, depending on whether the regulator believes there is a reasonable chance of preserving the company through commutations, i.e., settlements of large claims, or reinsurance arrangements, or selling books of business, or selling the entire company including its licenses.[2] In California the term for insurer rehabilitation proceedings is "Conservation", and the official appointed by the Superior Court to administer the proceeding is the "Conservator".[3]

It is critical to keep in mind that insurance companies domiciled in a U.S. state cannot be debtors under the federal Bankruptcy Code and all proceedings must occur in state courts.[4] Certain U.S.-situs property of non-U.S. insurers, however, can be administered in a Chapter 15 proceeding by federal Bankruptcy Court, and the Bankruptcy Court can enjoin suits seeking to recover such property. However, where the alien insurer has made a deposit or set up a trust in order to comply with a state insurance regulation so that it can operate as a reinsurer or as a surplus line insurer, the federal Bankruptcy Court has no jurisdiction over that property.[5]

On various grounds, such as, actual insolvency, or being in a "hazardous financial condition" or even willful non-compliance with applicable insurance laws, state insurance departments are allowed by statute to seize control over "delinquent" domestic insurance companies.[6] By state court order, in a public proceeding after notice to the insurer and a chance for the insurer to contest the petition, a state insurance department takes over management of insurer, and the Commissioner of Insurance (or equivalent state official) acts as rehabilitator (or conservator in California), but the insurer retains title to assets and the insurer continues in existence. This procedure is used when there is some chance the

---

[2]   *See, e.g.,* N.H. Rev. Stat. 404-F:5 and 404-F:6.
[3]   Cal. Ins. Code § 1011 *et seq.*
[4]   11 U.S.C. § 109.
[5]   11 U.S.C. § 1501(d).
[6]   *See, e.g.,* N.Y. Ins. L. § 7402; Tenn. Code § 56-9-301.

insurer can be re-structured or regain financial health through a sale of books of business or through reinsurance, and then become solvent again.

Almost always the rehabilitator stops paying claims except relatively small ones, and the policyholder or third-party claimant must file a claim with the court by the "bar date" which is set by the court at the request of the rehabilitator. The "bar date" is the court-ordered deadline for filing claims against the insurer's estate. A rehabilitator appointed by the court "steps into the shoes" of the delinquent insurance company such that all policy defenses which the insurer could have asserted are now available to the rehabilitator—e.g., non-payment of premium, exclusions, limits, sub-limits, misrepresentations by the policyholder during the under-writing process, or non-cooperation by the policyholder or claimant in the underlying litigation. The state court supervising the rehabilitation proceeding determines if the claim should be "allowed", and if the claim is contested, the court can order that a pre-trial discovery and ultimately a trial can occur.

A rehabilitator is authorized to propose a Plan of Rehabilitation which often provides for reduced payments on allowed policyholder claims as a means of preserving the company. Unlike Chapter 11 in federal bank-ruptcy proceedings, state insurer receivership laws do not permit any vote by policyholders and creditors on the Plan. Instead, interested parties are allowed a hearing on the proposed Plan at which they can submit testi-mony. If the supervising state court finds that the Plan is generally fair and reasonable, it can approve it.[7]

Almost always a rehabilitation plan will involve reducing the amount the insurer will have to pay on a policy to policyholders and claimants. The U.S. Supreme Court has held that, as a matter of federal constitu-tional law, policyholders are not denied due process if the amount they receive in a rehabilitation is at least as much as they would receive if the insurer were liquidated.[8]

---

[7]   *See, e.g.,* Utah Code § 31A-27a-303.

[8]   *Neblett v. Carpenter,* 305 U.S. 297 (1938); *see also Foster v. Mutual Fire, Marine & Inland Ins. Co.,* 531 Pa. 598, 614 A.2d 1086 (Pa. Sup. Ct. 1992) *cert. den.* 506 U.S. 1080 (1993).

III.   LIQUIDATION

When there is no reasonable chance of rehabilitation, the regulator, as liquidator, petitions the state court supervising the proceeding for an Order of Liquidation, and if the petition is granted, the liquidator takes title to insurer's assets and operates insurer in liquidation. An insurer placed into liquidation often is insolvent, i.e., its liabilities exceed its admitted assets, but depending on the domestic state law, the insurer need not actually be insolvent to go into either rehabilitation/conservation or liquidation. Grounds for either type of proceeding are very broad, e.g., "continued operations hazardous to policyholders".[9] State courts routinely show deference to regulators' petitions for rehabilitation/conservation or liquidation.[10]

In both rehabilitations and liquidations, at the start of the proceeding the state courts enjoin all attempts to collect on the insurer's policies and all attempts to recover on the insurer's property except by filing a claim in that court, or in an "ancillary" state court proceeding. Claims are usually adjudicated in "ancillary" proceedings when the insurer has assets in the ancillary state, such as a statutorily required deposit of cash or marketable securities needed to obtain a license. "Ancillary" rehabilitators and liquidators have statutory authority to pay allowed claims from *those* assets but then are required to transfer any excess assets to the domestic rehabilitator or liquidator.[11]

In liquidations, claims are subject to a strict priority regime: after administrative claims, e.g., the fees of lawyers and other professionals retained by the liquidator are paid, only then are the allowed claims of policyholders and claimants paid, but, typically, with no interest amounts added to the amount of the claim, no matter how many years or even decades elapse until payment. Those policyholders and claimants have priority over general creditors and must be paid in full before general creditors, *including reinsurers*, are paid anything.[12] Like a rehabilitator

---

[9] *See, e.g.,* N.Y. Ins. L. § 7404 (incorporating all grounds that could be invoked for rehabilitation); *but see* Mass. G.L. ch. 175 § 180C (requiring insolvency as a ground for liquidation).

[10] *See, e.g., Stewart v. Citizens Casualty Co.,* 34 A.D.2d 525 (1st. Dept.), *affd.* 27 N.Y.2d 685 (1970) *cert. denied,* 401 U.S. 910 (1971) (criteria for placing insurer into liquidation).

[11] *See, e.g.,* Mass. G.L. ch. 175, § 180E.

[12] *See, e.g.,* N.Y. Ins. L. §7434.

(or conservator), the liquidator of an insurer has all of the rights of the insurer to assert defenses on claims under policies the insurer had issued, but, likewise, is bound by a final, unappealable judgment against the insurer prior to the liquidation. If, for example, a policyholder or claimant has already obtained a final and unappealable judgment against the insurer by the date of liquidation, the liquidator is bound by the judgment just as the insurer would have been had no liquidation proceeding occurred.

Because reinsurers know that under state insurer liquidation priority laws they are unlikely to ever recover anything if the ceding insurer were liquidated—with all policyholder and claimant claims having to be paid *in full* first, and that almost never happens—reinsurance contracts routinely contain an "offset" clause allowing either the ceding company or the assuming reinsurer to offset amounts owed by the other party against the amounts they owe to that party. For example, if a ceding company owes reinsurance premium of $1 million to a reinsurer and the reinsurer owes the ceding company $ 2 million in losses, then upon the liquidation of the ceding company, under the "offset" clause the reinsurer can deduct $1 million from the amount it must pay the ceding insurer's liquidator. *Most states, but not all,* allow reinsurers to invoke "offset" clauses.[13]

Liquidators and rehabilitators and their staffs spend much of their time trying to collect from assuming reinsurers which may owe millions of dollars to the ceding insurer that has been placed into receivership. It typically takes years, even decades, for all the disputes with reinsurers to be resolved, usually through arbitration proceedings, but sometimes in protracted litigation to confirm or vacate arbitration awards. Almost all reinsurance contracts require that disputes between the parties be arbitrated instead of litigated in public court proceedings. Liquidators and rehabilitators also sell real estate owned by the insurer and marshal other assets to pay allowed claims according to the applicable state priority statute.

---

[13]   *See, e.g., Prudential Reinsurance Co. v. Superior Ct. (Garamendi)*, 3 Cal. 4th 1118, 842 P. 2d 48 (Cal. 1992), *Commissioner of Ins. v Munich Am. Reinsurance Co.*, 429 Mass. 140, 706 NE2d 694 (Mass. 1999) and *In re Midland Ins. Co.*, 79 N.Y.2d 253, 582 N.Y.S.2d 58 (N.Y. Ct. App. 1992) (allowing reinsurers to offset) *with Allendale Mutual Ins. Co. v. Melahn*, 773 F. Supp. 1283 (W.D. Mo. 1991) and *Foster v. Mutual Fire, Marine & Inland Ins. Co.*, 531 Pa. 598, 614 A.2d 1086 (Pa. Sup. Ct. 1992) *cert. den.* 506 U.S. 1080 (1993) (denying reinsurers the right to offset).

As noted in Chapter 5, liquidators, and rehabilitators of insurance companies in every state can invoke one favorable principle in attempting to collect from reinsurers: the reinsurer must pay the liquidator or rehabilitator whatever it owes, even though the insurance company in receivership, because of lack of funds, has not yet paid the direct policyholder or claimant on the reinsured policy. This principle is codified in every state in statutes that require every licensed company seeking credit on its financial statements for the reinsurance to include an "insolvency clause" in its reinsurance contracts by which the reinsurer agrees to pay any liquidator or rehabilitator of the company "without diminution" by reason of the company's insolvency.[14]

Although reinsurers are in the category of general creditors and must therefore try to protect themselves through an "offset" clause if the particular state law permits, lenders who make secured loans are in a much better legal position. Banks and other lenders who have made secured loans to insurers subsequently placed into rehabilitation or liquidation need to follow the laws addressing secured loans.[15] A secured lender is allowed to foreclose on the security but must first obtain an order from the state court supervising the proceeding which grants relief from the broad court injunction issued as part of the order of liquidation or rehabilitation against any attempt to recover on the insurer's property.

Once the secured creditor has obtained such a relief order, it may foreclose on the security. If there is a deficiency between the value of the security as of the date of liquidation and the amount owed by the insurer, the creditor may file an unsecured claim for the balance, but that claim is extremely unlikely to be paid because all policyholders and claimants must first be paid in full under state insurer liquidation priority laws. Every U.S. state accords favorable treatment to secured creditors in insurer rehabilitation and liquidation proceedings, provided they first obtain an order from the state court allowing them to foreclose on the security.

One other class of creditors is also in a favorable position if the insurer being rehabilitated or liquidated underwrote life insurance and annuities and offered "separate accounts". These are policies and annuity contracts, particularly group annuities that are bought by pension plans to fund pension obligations, which are backed, not by the general assets of

---

[14]   *See, e.g.,* N.Y. Ins. L. § 1308; Wyo. Stat. § 26-5-115.
[15]   *See, e.g.,* 36 Okla. Stat.§1919(D).

the insurer, but, rather, by specific pools of investments allocated to that separate account. The advantage of being a policyholder or an annuitant covered by a "separate account" is that the insurer's payments under the policy and annuity contract are made only from those investments, not from the general assets which are chargeable with all of the insurer's liabilities to other policyholders and contract holders and all other creditors.

For a life insurance company to be able to establish and maintain one or more "separate accounts", it must first secure regulatory approval in each state in which it proposes to underwrite policies and annuity contracts covered by such "separate accounts". That process typically requires advance regulatory approval of a Plan of Operation for the separate account, a credible set of actuarial projections made by a qualified, expert life actuary, and compliance with a detailed set of regulations governing investment and disposition of assets that will fund the separate account.[16]

For policyholders and annuity contract holders who are not covered from a "separate account", they must carefully consider whether a payment from the insurer within a specified time before rehabilitation or liquidation proceedings would constitute a *voidable preference*. Just as in federal bankruptcy, state laws allow a rehabilitator (conservator) or liquidator of an insurer to recover from a creditor who has received a preference by obtaining more on a pre-proceeding debt during a specified period prior to the proceeding than the creditor would be entitled to in the proceeding.[17] The applicable period will be specified in the preference statute applicable to insurer liquidations and rehabilitations in that particular state, but typically runs from one year prior to the date of the liquidation petition.

Whenever a lender or other counterparty is negotiating a settlement with an insurer for which there is a realistic possibility that the insurer will be in such a proceeding within the next year or two, expert counsel should be consulted on the law of preferences in insurer receiverships in the insurer's domicile. If the domestic regulator of the insurer is encouraging the counterparty such as a major policyholder, to conclude a settlement with the insurer, keep in mind that the statements and positions taken by the regulator are not legally binding on the rehabilitator or liquidator, even if the Commissioner of Insurance as regulator is the same

---

[16]   *See, e.g.,* N.Y. Ins. L. § 4240 and 11 N.Y.C.R.R. Part 50.
[17]   *See, e.g.,* Tex. Ins. Code § 443.204.

person as the subsequently appointed Commissioner as Liquidator.[18] Thus, a commutation or a settlement with the insurer within a year or two of a liquidation or rehabilitation proceeding may still be considered a voidable preference under the applicable state law, even if the domestic regulator of the insurance company explicitly encouraged the parties to execute a commutation or settlement agreement.

BOX 6.1   PRACTICAL TIP FOR PRACTITIONERS

In a situation involving a significant settlement with an insurer facing an uncertain financial future, the regulator should be asked to state in writing that, to the extent permitted by law, it would be the position of the Department (or equivalent state agency) administering the liquidation or rehabilitation of the insurer that the amount paid in settlement received regulatory approval, was fair and reasonable, and would not be deemed a voidable preference under the state insurer receivership laws. That statement, if provided by the regulator, is not dispositive on the state court supervising the receivership, but it would make it more difficult for the rehabilitator or liquidator to later argue, and for the state court to find, that a voidable preference occurred.

IV.   STATE INSURANCE GUARANTY FUNDS

Every state requires licensed insurers to pay assessments to fund the guaranty fund which covers claims asserted by residents of the state against insolvent insurers. Life and health insurance companies pay assessments for state guaranty funds covering life and health insurance claims, while property and casualty insurers pay assessments to fund the guaranty fund covering property and casualty claims. Insurers that fail to pay assessments can have their license suspended or revoked or be subject to specified monetary penalties.[19]

---

[18]   *Corcoran v. Frank B. Hall & Co.*, 145 A.D. 2d 165 (N.Y. App. Div. 1989) (even if the same actual human being, the Superintendent as regulator is a separate and distinct legal person as the Superintendent as liquidator).

[19]   *See, e.g.*, Mass. G.L. ch. 175 § 146B (life and health guaranty fund statute); Mass. G.L. ch. 175D (property and casualty fund statute).

The assessments are calculated based on how much premium the particular insurer wrote in the state in the preceding year or specified number of years as a proportion of the total premium during that period written by all assessed insurers—with the insurers writing the most premium paying the biggest assessments. Insurers are allowed to take into account the amount of assessments in determining their rates and state tax liabilities.[20]

Guaranty funds are governed by directors elected by the licensed insurers paying the assessments implementing a plan of operation approved by the state insurance department. The funds work closely with rehabilitators (conservators) and liquidators, and their respective staffs, to pay *timely* and *valid* claims up to the policy limits, but not more than a statutory maximum amount depending on the state and the kind of insurance. For example, the New York Property and Casualty Security Fund will pay up to $1 million on a covered property or casualty claim involving a New York risk while the Alabama Insurance Guaranty Association will not pay more than $300,000 on a similar property or casualty claim involving an Alabama risk.[21]

Numerous states have adopted limits on payments from guaranty funds to wealthy claimants typically defined as "high net worth" claimants. For example, the Massachusetts Insurers Insolvency Fund and a similar fund in Indiana will *not* pay a property claim to a person or an entity with a net worth of more than $25 million (including the net worth of subsidiary and affiliated companies).[22]

To recover from a state insurance guaranty fund, the claim must be timely submitted within the deadline set forth in the state guaranty fund law or, depending on the state, the "bar date" set by the state court supervising the liquidation on the motion of the liquidator. The guaranty fund and the producer listed as having sold the policy can be ordered to notify policyholders of the liquidation and the procedures and deadline for submitting claims.[23] The fund is allowed to assert any policy defenses which the insurer could have asserted on the claim, and the claimant must assign her, his or its rights under the fund to the extent of the fund's payment. The liquidator must treat the guaranty fund as a second priority creditor

---

[20] *See, e.g.,* Mass. G.L. ch. 175D; https://www.tax.ny.gov/bus/ct/life_ins_credit.htm.

[21] *See* N.Y. Ins. L. § 7603 and Alabama Code § 27-42-8.

[22] *See, e.g.,* Mass. G.L. ch. 175D (17); Indiana Code § 27-6-8-11.5.

[23] *See, e.g.,* Indiana Code § 27-6-8-9.

entitled to share along with policyholders in the distributed assets of the estate on a *pro rata* basis.[24]

V.   NEW APPROACHES TO PREVENTING INSURER REHABILITATIONS AND LIQUIDATIONS

In the last several years some states have adopted laws allowing licensed insurers to transfer their unprofitable or undesired books of business to domestic licensed insurers upon regulatory, and in certain states judicial approval, without having to obtain the consent of each policyholder. In 2018 Oklahoma adopted an Insurance Business Transfer Act,[25] allowing an Oklahoma licensed insurer to transfer any part of its insurance or reinsurance business to an Oklahoma domestic insurer and have their direct policies or reinsurance contracts novated, with the transferee Oklahoma insurer being substituted for the transferring company on the policies or contracts, and the transferring company having no further liabilities to direct policyholders or ceding insurers on those direct policies or reinsurance contracts.

The Oklahoma Act requires a detailed transfer plan and actuarial projections and other financial information be approved, first, by the domestic regulator of the transferring insurer, then by the Oklahoma Insurance Department, then by an Oklahoma court after policyholders or ceding insurers are notified and have the opportunity to object. However, those parties do not have the power to veto or opt out of the transfer, and the Oklahoma court must approve the transfer and novation if it finds that the interests of policyholders and claimants will not be materially harmed.

Somewhat similarly Rhode Island adopted a statute and Insurance Department regulations allowing a transfer and novation of certain property/casualty books of business following regulatory approval of a transfer plan accompanied by an expert's opinion favoring the proposed transaction, approval by the domestic regulator of the transferring company, approval of the Rhode Island Insurance Department, and the approval of a Rhode Island court after affording policyholders, claimants and/or ceding insurers the opportunity to present objections. The insurance or reinsurance business to be transferred must be in "run-off"

---

[24]   *See, e.g.,* Mass. G.L. ch. § 175D (8).
[25]   36 Okla. Stat. § 1681 *et seq.*

status, i.e., no policies are being issued or renewed, but existing policies are being kept in force to their respective expiration dates.[26] Connecticut also enacted a law in 2017 authorizing the division of domestic insurers into two or more new insurers to which existing policies are allocated, and the original insurer is relieved of any obligations under those policies after the division *if* the domestic regulator approves a plan of division.[27]

---

[26] R.I. Stat. Chapter 27-14.5.
[27] Conn. Pub. Acts 17-2(2017).

7. How state insurance regulators supervise the market conduct of insurance companies and insurance professionals

In the last 25 years, U.S. state insurance regulators have become much more concerned with how insurance companies and insurance professionals have treated their policyholders, claimants, and customers than in previous decades when regulators—although certainly not indifferent to marketplace abuses—tended mainly to focus on the financial condition of insurance companies. State insurance departments in the U.S. are headed by women and men who have either been elected by the voters themselves, as in California and North Carolina, or appointed by elected Governors as in most states. Therefore, the political pressures to safeguard the rights of the insurance-buying public have become increasingly intense, and insurance commissioners must now compete in the court of public opinion with politically ambitious attorneys general—many of whom have targeted insurance companies and large producers for enforcement proceedings—to be perceived as championing consumer interests. In this chapter we shall consider the various ways in which U.S. state insurance regulators supervise the market conduct of licensed insurers and producers.

I.   SUPERVISING THE MARKET CONDUCT OF INSURANCE COMPANIES

1.   General Restrictions and Prohibitions on Underwriting and Claims Handling Practices

States have enacted numerous statutes and regulations for the purpose of ensuring that insurers treat prospective customers, existing policyholders, and current claimants fairly. Some examples of these provisions are:

- laws *prohibiting unfair discrimination* in underwriting and rating, e.g., based on race, sex or national origin;[1] *but note that not all risk discrimination is considered unfair*—based on decades of actuarial data, U.S. state insurance regulators routinely allow women to be charged less for life insurance, and allow car owners with the best driving records to be charged less than other drivers with more accidents and/or traffic infractions;[2]
- laws *requiring insurers to acknowledge claims within a specified time period* and either pay the claim, deny the claim, or ask for more information about the claim within specified time periods;[3]
- laws prohibiting *any misleading advertising* of insurance policies;[4]
- except to some extent in California, and to a lesser extent in Florida, laws *prohibiting insurers and agents from offering rebates* unless plainly specified in the policy, which must be filed or not objected to by regulators—an event which happens extremely rarely outside of those two states;[5]
- laws which *prohibit insurance companies and producers from conditioning the sale* of another product or service on the purchase of insurance;[6]
- laws requiring that *rates be filed* and, depending on the type of policy and the state, not objected to, *or*, in the case of certain types of coverage, such as personal auto insurance, actually approved;[7]

---

[1]   *See, e.g.,* Mass G.L. ch. 175 § 22E.
[2]   *See, e.g.,* N.Y. Ins. L. L. § 2334.
[3]   *See, e.g.,* Ohio Admin. Code § 3901-1-54.
[4]   *See, e.g.,* Cal. Ins. Code § 790.03.
[5]   *See, e.g.,* Tex. Ins. Code § 541.056.
[6]   *See, e.g.,* N.Y. Ins. L. §§ 2324, 4224.
[7]   *See, e.g.,* Ark. Ins. Code §§ 23-67-201 *et seq.*

- laws requiring that *policy forms be filed*, and, depending on the state and type of policy, either not objected to or actually approved by regulators;[8]
- laws requiring that the *language of policies be in* "plain English", using a metric for readability known as the "Flesch test" to determine how comprehensible the policy terms are to an ordinary consumer.[9]
- laws restricting the right of insurers to cancel or non-renew policies.[10]
- laws requiring insurers that wish to withdraw from a state's market to obtain regulatory approval for a *detailed Plan of Withdrawal*.[11]
- laws *requiring that insurers provide specified coverages*, especially in health insurance policies; and[12]
- *laws prohibiting insurers from requiring claimants to have their damaged motorcars repaired at particular repair shops*, but insurers are allowed to make recommendations to policyholders and claimants of particular shops under specified conditions.[13]

In addition to these kinds of prohibitions and restrictions, another typical prohibition imposed on licensed insurers in most states led to federal preemption of certain state insurance regulations about four decades ago. These state rules barred insurance companies from offering group liability insurance coverage for manufacturers seeking product liability coverage, and, later, doctors, lawyers, architects, and other professionals seeking malpractice insurance. Those restrictive state rules largely emanated from the concerns of licensed insurance producers who feared that pervasive group insurance would reduce the commissions they were receiving on individually issued policies.

In 1981 and again in 1986 Congress sought to address the affordability and availability problems in the market for commercial liability insurance. The result was the Product Liability Risk Retention Act of 1981 and the Liability Risk Retention Act of 1986. These federal laws broadly and explicitly preempted any state laws which prohibited insurers from

---

[8] *See, e.g.,* New York Dept. Fin. Serv. Guidance https://www.dfs.ny.gov/apps_and_licensing/property_insurers/rate_form_filings (last visited July 11, 2023);

[9] *See, e.g.,* Nev. Rev. Stat. § 687B.124.

[10] *See, e.g.,* Pa. Code § tit. 31 § 59.1 *et seq.*.

[11] *See, e.g.,* Cal. Ins. Code §§ 1070–1076.

[12] *See, e.g.,* Missouri Ins. Code §§ 376.1224. 1 *et seq. (*mandating coverage in specified group health plans for autism spectrum disorders).

[13] *See, e.g.,* Cal. Ins. Code § 758.5.

offering commercial liability coverage on a group basis by allowing entities in a similar trade, business or profession—notwithstanding any state prohibition to the contrary—to form "risk retention groups" which act like direct insurers, but do not need to undergo the traditional state insurer licensing process, and also to form "purchasing groups" to obtain commercial liability insurance on a group basis from licensed insurance companies.[14] Risk retention groups are discussed in Chapter 4.

States have begun to permit group insurance for a handful of property/casualty coverages, while continuing to allow group life and health insurance much more broadly. For example, New York permits group coverage for property and even liability insurance obtained in conjunction with using a credit card, and, more recently, allows group motor vehicle coverage for persons participating in "peer-to-peer" shared automobile rentals, such as, e.g., Zipcar.[15]

Group property/casualty insurance, however, is still largely prohibited, outside the scope of these two federal laws that only deal with *liability insurance* policies. For example, it is still illegal in most states for a licensed insurer to cover ordinary commercial property risks—e.g., fire, theft, boiler and machinery, embezzlement, or property damage from a hurricane, volcano or earthquake—on a group basis where the members of the group are not affiliated companies and do not face exposure on a joint and several basis.[16]

Although states still restrict group insurance in the property insurance marketplace, they have increasingly permitted admitted companies to offer "mass merchandized" policies which are individually underwritten and separately issued to each policyholder, but which are marketed on a group basis—e.g., advertised to all members of a professional organization or all alumni of a particular university.[17]

---

[14]   15 U.S.C. §§ 3902, 3904.
[15]   N.Y. Ins. L. §§ 3442, 3458.
[16]   *See, e.g.,* Idaho Code Ann. § 41-1317(1); N.Y. Ins. L. 3435 (allowing group property insurance only for public entities and certain non-profit organizations) and Opinion of the Office of General Counsel 06-04-08 accessible at: https://www.dfs.ny.gov/insurance/ogco2006/rg060408.htm (last visited July 11, 2023).
[17]   *See, e.g.,* 11 N.Y.C.R.R. Part 153 (prescribing regulations for marketing "quasi-group" property/casualty policies in New York).

2.   Regulating Premium Rates

State insurance regulators evaluate the premium rates used by licensed carriers under several basic, somewhat contradictory, criteria:

- rates may not be excessive;
- rates may not be inadequate; and
- rates may not be unfairly discriminatory.

Not all rates need to be formally approved, however.[18] In general, rates for coverage of personal private passenger motorcars, the rates businesses must pay for workers' compensation insurance, and rates for homeowners'/renters' insurance typically require actual regulatory approval, although rates for commercial property/casualty coverage do not.[19]

State insurance departments utilize three types of procedures for evaluating insurance rates:

- *actual approval* for certain types of insurance, mainly for "personal lines" as stated above;
- "file and use" for life insurance and annuities and certain specified types of commercial insurance policies, depending on the state, allowing the insurer to use the filed rates, if regulators do not object within a specified period, usually between 15 and 30 days;[20] and
- "use and file" typically, but not always, for commercial insurance policies where the insurer is allowed to use the rate until and unless the regulator objects.[21]

3.   Regulation of Policy Forms

Similarly, policy forms must either receive actual approval, or be deemed approved if filed and regulators make no objection within a specified period.[22] States have issued detailed guides and checklists to assist insur-

---

[18]   *See, e.g.,* O.C.G.A. § 33-9-4; 36 Okla. Stat. § 36-90.
[19]   *See, e.g.,* N.Y. Ins. L. § 2305 (listing the types of insurance for which actual approval is required in New York).
[20]   *See, e.g.,* Alaska Stat. § 21.39.041.
[21]   *See, e.g.,* N.J.S.A. § 17:29AA-5; Fla. Code § 627.0651.
[22]   *See, e.g.,* Ariz. Rev. Stat. § 20-398.

ers in making rate and form filings.[23] State insurance departments typically require that when filing a proposed policy form the insurer certify that the filing complies with applicable state laws.[24]

Since 2007 a large number of states have joined the Interstate Insurance Product Regulation Commission, called the Interstate Insurance Compact, which allows insurers underwriting life insurance, annuities, disability income and long-term care insurance in 45 states to make one set of form filings for particular products, and if the Commission approves the filing—utilizing numerous product standards adopted by the Commission—the insurer may use the form in those 45 states. Note, however, that several populous states—California, New York and Florida—do not participate in the Compact.

4.   Enforcing Insurer Market Conduct Laws

States examine insurers for compliance with market conduct laws, often at the same time they are conducting financial solvency examinations.[25] States routinely impose fines for non-compliance, such as issuing policies with unapproved forms and/or rates or failing to process valid claims in a timely manner.[26]

States also receive and consider complaints by policyholders and claimants as to market conduct and can impose penalties for non-compliance. In some cases regulators can require the insurer to pay policyholders and claimants according to the policy terms.[27]

---

[23]   *See, e.g.,* Fla. OIR Life and Health Product Review: https://www.floir.com/Sections/LandH/ProductReview/is_lhfr_LnHnFnR.aspx (last visited July 11, 2023) and Fla. OIR Property and Casualty Product Review: https://www.floir.com/Sections/PandC/ProductReview/Bureau_PC_FormsRates.aspx (last visited July 11, 2023).

[24]   *See, e.g.,* https://insurance.utah.gov/wp-content/uploads/220AHFilingCertification.pdf (last visited July 11, 2023).

[25]   *See, e.g.,* Conn. Ins. Dept. Market Conduct Examination Reports: https://www.catalog.state.ct.us/cid/portalApps/examinations.aspx (last visited July 11, 2023).

[26]   *See, e.g.,* N.Y. Dept. of Fin. Serv. Press Releases: https://www.dfs.ny.gov/reports_and_publications/press_releases/pr202205201; https://www.dfs.ny.gov/reports_and_publications/press_releases/pr202011031 (last visited July 11, 2023).

[27]   *See, e.g.,* Colorado Div. of Ins. Annual Report of Complaints Against Insurers 2019-20 https://drive.google.com/drive/folders/1tdS1FcgUF_n-gRd5e9QznBet2YeWWOGL (last visited July 11, 2023).

States can require insurers to file specified market conduct information as part of a special report.[28] In 2005 New York and other states invoking this type of law began to investigate whether life insurers were failing to pay unclaimed death benefits even though they knew that the insured person had died because they stopped paying annuity benefits to that person. State insurance regulators recovered millions of dollars for beneficiaries who did not know that they were eligible to receive death benefits.[29]

II.   SUPERVISING THE MARKET CONDUCT OF PRODUCERS AND OTHER INSURANCE PROFESSIONALS

States regulate the market conduct of agents and brokers, and other licensed insurance producers, in various ways, including through:

* laws *requiring producers to place premium funds in fiduciary accounts* which cannot be used for any purpose other than forwarding premiums to insurers;[30]
* laws *requiring producers to disclose to customers how insurers will compensate them*, and in New York, requiring producers—on request of the customer—to calculate actual commissions or reasonably estimate commissions that are contingent on volume, longevity and profitability;[31]
* laws requiring producers who wish to charge their clients a fee for their service to have a *written agreement specifying the amount of the fee*;[32]
* laws which require producers to determine if the purchase of an annuity is "suitable" for the customer based on the customer's particular financial needs and status and requiring producers to give

---

[28]   *See, e.g.,* N.Y. Ins. L. § 308.
[29]   *See, e.g.,* https://www.lexisnexis.com/legalnewsroom/insurance/b/insurancelaw/posts/settlement-reached-in-death-master-case-with-new-york-life-insuramce-company (last visited July 11, 2023).
[30]   *See, e.g.,* O.C.G.A. § 33-23-35; https://www.dfs.ny.gov/system/files/documents/2022/03/da20220304.pdf (last visited July 11, 2023).
[31]   *See, e.g.,* 11 N.Y.C.R.R. Part 30; Oregon Admin. Rules § 836-071-0260.
[32]   *See, e.g.,* Cal Code Reg. 2189.1 *et seq*; N.Y. Ins. L. § 2119.

specified disclosures that replacement of an annuity could involve substantial surrender fees and other disadvantages;[33]

- New York adopted a similar rule for *life insurance agents* in 2018, requiring them to *act in the best interest of their customers*, even if the result is lower commissions paid to them;[34] and
- laws requiring producers and adjusters to implement cybersecurity policies and procedures.[35]

III.   THE ROLE OF U.S. STATE ATTORNEYS GENERAL IN SUPERVISING INSURANCE MARKET CONDUCT

Beginning in 2004 and led by the New York State Attorney General, the attorneys general in various U.S. states became *de facto* insurance regulators enforcing state antitrust and consumer protection laws against insurance companies and insurance producers. Major insurance producers such as Marsh and large insurance companies such as ACE agreed to pay millions of dollars to New York and other states for improperly steering customers to insurers and bid rigging.[36] It has now become routine for attorney general offices in New York, Massachusetts, Texas and other states to announce significant enforcement actions affecting the insurance industry.[37]

---

[33]   NAIC Suitability in Annuities Model Regulation adopted in some states: https://content.naic.org/cipr-topics/annuity-suitability-best-interest-standard; https://www.jdsupra.com/legalnews/recent-state-fiduciary-and-best-5126918/ (last visited July 11, 2023).

[34]   *See* 11 N.Y.C.R.R. Part 224.

[35]   *See* 11 N.Y.C.R.R. Part 500.

[36]   *See, e.g.,* https://ag.ny.gov/press-release/2006/ace-settles-bid-rigging -probe (last visited July 11, 2023).

[37]   *See, e.g.,* https://ag.ny.gov/press-release/2022/attorney-general-james -secures-relief-patients-illegally-charged-ambulance; https://www.mass.gov/ news/insurance-company-to-pay-625000-to-resolve-claims-of-unlawful-and -deceptive-sales-of-health-plans; https://texasattorneygeneral.gov/news/releases/ ag-paxton-announces-start-wells-fargo-consumer-redress-review-program   (last visited July 11, 2023).

BOX 7.1   PRACTICAL TIP FOR PRACTITIONERS

If you represent a client before a state insurance department market conduct unit and/or state Attorney General's office seeking to sanction your client for alleged illegal market conduct, do *not* expect any settlement agreement to provide that your client acted unintentionally or made a good faith mistake. Instead, seek to minimize the amount of monetary penalties to be imposed on your client by thoroughly researching how regulators in that state have dealt with similar illegal conduct of other companies by reviewing all publicly available press releases of prior enforcement actions against those other companies. Often, these are accompanied by the actual Consent Agreements or Stipulations signed by regulators and/or assistant attorneys general which concluded the respective enforcement actions. Argue that, absent a change in the applicable law, your client should not be penalized more harshly than a similarly situated company which executed such a Consent Agreement or Stipulation.

8. How the U.S. federal government and state insurance regulators supervise health insurance

The field of health insurance regulation and the interplay between state and federal laws in the United States is so detailed and complex that this primer can only provide a high-level, but hardly exhaustive, summary of the key statutes and principal regulatory concepts in that field.

I.   MAJOR FEDERAL LAWS DIRECTLY PROVIDING HEALTH INSURANCE BENEFITS

Among the major federal statutes which provide for the U.S. federal government to directly provide health insurance benefits are the following:

- Social Security disability benefits;[1]
- Medicare health coverage for persons 65 and older;[2]
- Medicaid, a joint federal and state income-based program;[3]
- Veterans' hospital, medical and nursing home benefits;[4]
- Children's Health Insurance Program;[5]
- Special Fund under the Longshore and Harbor Workers' Compensation Act;[6]
- Indian Health Care Improvement Act of 1976.[7]

---

[1]   42 U.S.C. §§ 401–433 and 42 U.S.C. §§ 1381–1385.
[2]   42 U.S.C. § 1395 *et seq.*
[3]   42 U.S.C. § 1396 *et seq.*
[4]   38 U.S.C. § 1701 *et seq.*
[5]   42 U.S.C. § 1397dd *et seq.*
[6]   33 U.S.C. § 944.
[7]   25 U.S.C. § 1601 *et seq.* and the Snyder Act of 192—*see* 25 U.S.C. 13.

II. PRINCIPAL FEDERAL LAWS WHICH REGULATE HEALTH INSURANCE

In Chapter 2 we examined how under the McCarran-Ferguson Act Congress retained its power to regulate interstate commerce by enacting legislation that specifically related to the business of insurance. Listed below are several federal laws, enacted since 1985, which expressly address the market conduct of health insurance companies, but in some of these laws, Congress has chosen not to completely divest U.S. state insurance regulators of authority.

1. Consolidated Omnibus Budget Reconciliation Act of 1985 ("COBRA")[8]

The COBRA law allows employees of a "qualifying employer"—one with at least 20 employees—to continue group health coverage for up to 18 months (29 months if found to be disabled by Social Security Administration, and 36 months for an employee's divorcing spouse or widow) if certain "qualifying events" occur causing a loss of group coverage. Among the specified "qualifying events" are:

(1) the death of the covered employee;
(2) the voluntary or involuntary termination or a reduction in hours as a result of resignation, discharge (except for "gross misconduct") layoff, strike or lockout, medical leave, or slowdown in business operations;
(3) divorce or legal separation that terminates the ex-spouse's eligibility for benefits; or
(4) a dependent child reaching the age at which he or she is no longer covered.

For the coverage to continue the employee must pay 100 percent of the premium previously paid by both the employer and the employee for the previous group coverage, *plus* an administrative charge of 2 percent. COBRA does not apply if the employer's group health plan has been terminated or if the employer goes out of business causing the group health plan to terminate.

---

[8] 29 U.S.C. Part 6

2.   The Health Insurance Portability and Accountability Act of 1996 (HIPAA)[9]

In 1996 Congress passed and President Clinton signed the HIPAA into law. This statute regulates coverage of pre-existing conditions by group health plans, mandates the use of electronic health records in certain specified situations, and, most significantly, prohibits the unauthorized release of non-public, personally identifiable health information with certain specified exceptions, such as (i) release to law enforcement authorities in investigations and prosecutions, and (ii) treatment, payment, and health care operations.

3.   Genetic Information Non-Discrimination Act of 2008[10]

This 2008 statute prohibits *health insurers* from requiring or requesting genetic testing as part of underwriting or in setting premium rates. The law, however, does not apply to life, disability income or long-term care insurance. The law expressly provides that a health care provider performing services under a health insurance plan may request a covered individual to undergo genetic testing for treatment purposes, and that a health insurer may request a covered individual to undergo genetic testing for research purposes under specified conditions.

4.   Newborns' and Mothers' Health Protection Act of 1996.[11]

This 1996 enactment provides that *if* a maternity hospital stay is covered in a group health policy, *then* insurers must cover the hospital stay in connection with childbirth of at least 48 hours following a vaginal delivery or 96 hours following a delivery by cesarean section, unless the attending doctor in consultation with the mother agrees to a shorter hospital stay. The law also requires health insurers to notify beneficiaries of mandated benefits. Note that a rare "reverse preemption" provision included by the Congress makes this law inapplicable to health insurers already regulated under a similar state law.

---

[9]   42 U.S.C. § 300gg *et seq*, 29 U.S.C. § 1181 *et seq*., and 42 U.S.C. § 1320d *et seq.*

[10]   Public Law 110 – 233, Title I (2008).

[11]   29 U.S.C. § 1185.

5.   The Women's Health and Cancer Rights Act of 1998 [12]

If a health insurance policy covers a mastectomy, *then* certain specified benefits for breast reconstruction in connection with a mastectomy must be provided under the policy. As with the Newborns' and Mothers' Health Protection Act, this statute does not apply to health insurers if a similar state law already applies to them.

6.   Paul Wellstone and Pete Domenici Mental Health Parity and Addictions Equity Act of 2008 [13]

This 2008 law requires *group* health insurers, underwriting health plans covering 50 persons or more, to ensure that the "financial requirements" and "treatment limitations" that are applicable to mental health and substance abuse benefits are no more restrictive than the predominant financial requirements and treatment limitations for medical and surgical benefits covered by the plan. The statute also mandates parity in terms of total annual dollar limits, as well as aggregate lifetime benefits; and, further, the law requires that insurers provide specific information and reasons if reimbursement or payment for mental health or substance abuse treatment is denied.

This statute has a cost-savings provision favorable to health insurers: if in one plan year or in one policy year the increase in total costs for medical, surgical, mental health and substance abuse exceed specified percentages, then the law's requirements will not apply for the following year. It is important to note that this law does not mandate coverage of mental health and substance abuse treatment in group health plans, only that—*if* the plan provides some mental health and substance abuse coverage—*then* health insurers cannot ordinarily provide fewer benefits for such treatment as compared to coverage of physical injuries and ailments.

---

[12]   29 U.S.C. 1185b.
[13]   29 U.S.C. 1185a.

7.   **Patient Protection and Affordable Care Act of 2010 (known colloquially as "Obamacare" or "ACA")[14]**

This most well-known of the federal laws regulating health insurance in the U.S. was modeled significantly on a Massachusetts law proposed and implemented by then Republican Governor Mitt Romney. The key features of the ACA are:

1. *the so-called "individual mandate"* requiring Americans to have qualifying health insurance but, as of 2017, there is no penalty for non-compliance (26 U.S.C. § 5000A) (the original provision was narrowly upheld as a tax by the Supreme Court in 2012[15] and an attempt by certain Republican state attorneys general to declare the ACA unconstitutional because the penalty was repealed failed for lack of jurisdictional standing;[16] (The website of the Kaiser Family Foundation provides a wealth of timely and informative materials on health insurance regulation in the U.S. accessible at: https://www.kff .org (last visited July 12, 2023)
2. *creating state-based American Health Benefit Exchanges* through which individuals can purchase coverage, with premium and cost-sharing credits available to individuals/families with income between 133–400 percent of the federal poverty level, and separate exchanges through which small businesses can purchase coverage;
3. *requiring policies in the individual and small group market to cover* "essential health benefits" such as maternity, mental health/substance abuse, prescription drugs, emergency treatment, laboratory services, and certain preventive services;
4. *standardizing coverage for Exchange plans into tiers from bronze to platinum*, with deductibles and copays varying from plan to plan— platinum having the highest premium but relatively low deductibles

---

[14]   Public Law No. 111–148.

[15]   *National Federation of Independent Business v. Sebelius*, 567 U.S. 519 (2012); *see also* Kaiser Health Foundation monograph on the importance of the "individual mandate": https://www.kff.org/health-reform/perspective/is-a-death -spiral-inevitable-if-there-is-no-mandate/(last visited July 12, 2023).

[16]   *California v. Texas* (No. 19-840, June 17, 2021), accessible at: https:// www.supremecourt.gov/opinions/20pdf/19-840_6jfm.pdf (last visited July 12, 2023).

and copays—but all plans in a given tier will provide the same overall level of protection to consumers;

5. *prohibiting insurers from using* "pre-existing conditions" in under-writing and rating—a prohibition known as "guarantee issue and renewability"—but allowing insurers to use rating variations *if based on age* (limited to 3 to 1 ratio), *premium rating area, family composition, and tobacco use* (limited to 1.5. to 1 ratio) in the individual and the small group market and the Exchange;

6. *expanding the Medicaid program for persons within specified income limits in those states volunteering to share costs with the Federal government*, but Texas and Florida are among the minority of states refusing to do so as of 2023;

7. *requiring insurers to allow persons up to age 26 to be insured under their parents' or guardian's health insurance policy*;

8. *prohibiting individual and group health plans from placing annual and lifetime limits on the dollar value of coverage*;

9. *requiring insurers issuing qualified health insurance to have a pub-licly reported minimum "medical loss ratio"* of 80 percent for indi-vidual and small group policies—i.e., 80 percent of their premium income must be spent on health care claims and quality improvement, leaving the remaining 20 percent for administration, marketing, and profit—and 85 percent for large group policies, and require non-complying insurers to pay rebates to plan enrollees;

10. *requiring qualified health plans* participating in the Exchange to meet *marketing requirements*, have adequate provider networks, contract with essential community providers, contract with "navigators" to conduct outreach and enrollment assistance, be accredited with respect to performance on quality measures, use a uniform enrollment form and standard format to present plan information, and disclose in plain language information on claims payment policies, enrollment, disenrollment, number of claims denied, cost-sharing requirements, out-of-network policies, and enrollee rights;

11. *assessing employers*: those with 50 or more full-time employees that do not offer coverage and that do not have at least one full-time employee who receives a premium tax credit a fee of $2,000 per full-time employee, excluding the first 30 employees from the assessment; and employers with 50 or more full-time employees that offer coverage but have at least one full-time employee receiving a premium tax credit, will pay the lesser of $3,000 for each employee

receiving a premium credit or $2,000 for each full-time employee, excluding the first 30 employees from the assessment; and

12. *requiring employers with more than 200 employees to automatically enroll employees into health insurance plans offered by the employer*, but employees may opt out of coverage.

8.   Consolidated Appropriations Act of 2021[17]

This statute which became effective in 2022 prohibits medical providers from sending balance bills to patients who received out-of-network services after seeking emergency care, or were transported by an air ambulance, or when they received nonemergency care at an in-network hospital but were unknowingly treated by an out-of-network physician or laboratory. Under this law patients pay only the deductibles and copayment amounts that they would under the in-network terms of their insurance plans. Providers cannot legally hold patients responsible for the difference between those amounts and the higher fees they might like to charge. Instead, those providers will have to work out with insurers acceptable payments through an independent arbitration process if the parties cannot resolve a billing dispute. For the uninsured, for whom everything is out of network, the bill requires the Secretary of Health and Human Services to create a provider-patient bill dispute resolution process.

In *some* cases, however, physicians are allowed to balance-bill their patients, but they must get written consent in advance. In those cases, physicians must provide a cost estimate and get patient consent at least 72 hours before treatment. For shorter-turnaround situations, the bill requires that patients receive the consent information the day the appointment is made. This provision allows consumers to forfeit protection but only in *nonemergency* circumstances and, even in certain nonemergency situations, the law bars many types of providers from the practice. Anesthesiologists, for example, cannot seek a patient's consent to balance-bill for their services in an in-network facility, nor can radiologists, pathologists, neonatologists, assistant surgeons, or laboratories.

---

[17]   Title I (No Surprises Act) Public Law No. 116-260.

III.   STATE LAWS WHICH REGULATE HEALTH INSURANCE

As we have seen in Chapter 5, in the U.S. the individual states, not the federal government, regulate the solvency of health insurance companies using such tools as annual and quarterly financial statements, on-site examinations, annual risk based capital calculations, investment rules, annual actuarial certifications, annual Own Risk Solvency Assessments, annual parental Enterprise Risk Reports, credit for reinsurance rules, restrictions on investments, restrictions on "extraordinary dividends", and regulation of inter-company transactions. In addition, states have prescribed what health insurance policies must cover to be marketed as a particular type of health insurance policy, such as a "major medical" policy.[18] States continue to regulate the underwriting of, and rates for, health insurance, even after Congress enacted the ACA.[19]

States continue to regulate health insurance provider networks which can take the form of "health maintenance organizations" (HMO), "preferred provider organizations" (PPO), and "Exclusive provider organizations (EPO).[20] An HMO typically requires the insured to use designated providers in order for the services to be covered, (although some HMOs allow use of out-of-network providers under specified circumstances in "point of service" plans) while a PPO allows an insured to use any licensed provider but with a higher deductible or a higher co-insurance amount if the provider has not been designated by the insurer as a "preferred provider".

In regulating HMOs and PPOs, states have prescribed detailed rules for such topics as:

• how these organizations credential providers, i.e., allow them to join the insurer's provider network;

---

[18]   *See, e.g.,* Tex. Ins. Code § 1201.104 (authorizing Commissioner to set specific standards for various types of health insurance policies) and Tex. Admin. Code Rules §§ 3.3070–3.3079; Kansas Admin. Reg. § 40-4-29.

[19]   *See, e.g.,* N.Y. Ins. L. § 3232 (restrictions on using pre-existing conditions in underwriting health insurance); Iowa Ins. Code §§ 514A.13, 514A.14 (deemed approval of rates required before rates can go into effect, and rates must not be unreasonable).

[20]   *See, e.g.,* Wyoming Ins. Code, Chapter 34 (regulation of HMOs); Conn. G.S. §§ 38a–479aa *et seq.* (regulation of PPOs).

- standards for measuring how adequate the network in terms of number of in-network providers in proportion to number of insureds and metrics such as average wait times for appointments;
- standards for implementing quality assurance programs to maintain quality care;
- what provider contracts with the organizations must contain and must not contain, e.g., rules prohibiting a provider contract from preventing the provider from discussing treatment options with an insured ("anti-gag rules");
- how insureds can gain access to specialists;
- to what extent care given by a particular provider can continue after termination of the provider from the network; and
- how insureds can appeal adverse coverage decisions to an independent body ("external appeal laws").

States also license, or otherwise regulate, various professionals who work with health insurers, such as:

- *third-party administrators* who operate similar to adjusters and contract with health insurers to administer health plans and process claims.[21]
- *utilization review agents* who determine whether a particular service or treatment is "medically necessary" in order for the insurer or the third-party administrator to determine whether it is covered;[22]
- *pharmacy benefit managers* which act as intermediaries between pharmacies and health insurers in selecting and pricing covered drugs;[23]
- *accountable care organizations* which are comprised of doctors and/ or other health care providers and which agree to provide medical or other health services under contract with a licensed health insurer or HMO and bear some insurance risk by being compensated on a per capita, per patient basis—such that if the aggregate or individual cost of covered services exceeds the payment, the organization incurs a financial loss;[24] and

---

[21] *See, e.g.,* Ga. Code §§ 33-23-100 *et seq.*
[22] *See, e.g.,* N.Y. Ins. L. Art. 49.
[23] *See, e.g.,* Kentucky Rev. Stat. § 304.9-053; https://www.dfs.ny.gov/apps _and_licensing/pharmacy_benefit_managers (last visited July 12, 2023).
[24] *See, e.g.,* N.Y. Pub. Health L. Art. 29-E; 11 N.Y.C.R.R. Part 101.

• "navigators" who do not sell health insurance but who assist persons and businesses in finding suitable plans on the Exchanges set up by the ACA.[25]

IV. STATE INSURANCE REGULATORS AND COVID-19

The COVID-19 pandemic resulted in a number of state insurance regulations requiring health insurers to cover testing and treatment and prohibiting them from cancelling policies for non-payment during the pendency of a specified emergency period. For example, Massachusetts prohibited health insurers from charging deductibles and co-pays for COVID-19 *treatment*.[26] Additionally, some states strictly prohibited health insurers and HMOs from applying deductibles and co-pays for COVID-19 *tests*.[27] Other states, e.g., Pennsylvania, requested, but did not mandate, that health insurers waive cost-sharing for testing.

Several states have required health insurers to pay for "tele-health" remote services from doctors and other healthcare providers for treatment of COVID-19 if the policy covered services performed in person. (Insurers do not object because sometimes the cost is less than an actual office visit[28].)

---

[25] *See, e.g.,* https://insurance.mo.gov/otherlicensees/navigators.php (last visited July 12, 2023).

[26] Mass. DOI Bulletin 2020-04 and 2020-13.

[27] *See, e.g.,* Cal. Dept. of Ins. Bull. (March 5, 2020) and New Jersey (DOBI Bulletin 20-03).

[28] *See, e.g.,* N.Y. Ins. L. §§ 3217-h, 4306-g and N.Y. Pub. Health L. § 4406-g and N.Y. Dept. of Fin. Serv. Circular Letter No. 6 (March 15, 2020).

9.   U.S. insurance regulation heading into the global technological future

I.   TRENDS IN INTERNATIONAL INSURANCE REGULATION

The regulatory landscape confronting U.S. state insurance regulators, insurers and insurance professionals today looks far more global than even 20 years ago, and all three groups must stay abreast of *international* insurance regulatory developments. U.S. insurers and producers can be affected by developments in international insurance regulation in two ways:

First, if they do business in other counties, those developments will directly affect them. Second, even if they do not, regulators in the U.S. are increasingly in contact with, and to some extent influenced by, regulators from other countries, particularly the European Union (EU). The National Association of Insurance Commissioners (NAIC) is a member of the International Association of Insurance Supervisors (IAIS), and IAIS members regularly attend NAIC meetings. As a prime example of international insurance regulatory cooperation, financial solvency metrics, such as the mandatory annual risk-based capital calculation for insurers discussed in Chapter 5, were developed by U.S. regulators in coordination with regulators in other countries.

1.   Covered Agreements with the European Union and United Kingdom

Covered Agreements were executed in 2017 and 2018 between the U.S. Federal Insurance Office (FIO) and the EU and between the FIO and the United Kingdom (U.K.) which provide for:

(i)   exempting qualified reinsurers domiciled in the EU and U.K. from having to post collateral for reinsurance liabilities owed to U.S. ceding insurers, and

(ii)   exempting U.S. insurers doing business in the EU and U.K. from having to meet particular local presence and group capital requirements.[1]

By September 2022, as the Covered Agreements required, every U.S. jurisdiction adapted its credit for reinsurance rules to be fully in accord with these agreements.[2]

Before the Covered Agreements a state was able to require an unlicensed reinsurer domiciled in the U.K. or in an EU country, no matter how well capitalized and properly operated, to post collateral in a trust or letter of credit at a licensed U.S. bank equivalent to all of the reinsurer's liabilities owed to a domestic ceding insurer. Under the reinsurance rules that a U.S. state had to adopt by September, 2022 to be consistent with the Covered Agreements, any reinsurer domiciled in the EU or in the U.K. would be exempt from the onerous collateral requirement in that state which:

(i)   maintains a minimum amount of own-funds equivalent to $250 million;
(ii)   satisfies a solvency capital requirement (SCR) of 100 percent under the financial standards set by the EU; and
(iii) is domiciled in a country which meets specified standards of regulation,

would be exempt from that onerous collateral requirement in that state.

Additionally, the Covered Agreements provided for one "worldwide group capital calculation" by which the amount of capital of affiliated groups of insurance companies would be measured. This provision affects large insurers which operate through affiliated insurers in different countries. According to the NAIC, as of December 2022, only about half the states had adopted the Model Law developed by the NAIC which prescribed how the "worldwide group capital calculation" would be made. In contrast to the credit for reinsurance rules that could be federally preempted if a state had not acted to amend its law by September, 2022, the "group capital calculation" did not implicate possible federal preemp-

---

[1]   https://content.naic.org/cipr-topics/covered-agreement (last visited July 12, 2023).
[2]   https://home.treasury.gov/policy-issues/financial-markets-financial-institutions-and-fiscal-service/federal-insurance-office/covered-agreements/preemption-analysis(last visited July 12, 2023).

tion. The calculation would operate by default: namely, if a state did not adopt the NAIC Model by November, 2022, regulators in the EU would apply the most stringent measure under Solvency II for calculating how much capital the group of affiliated U.S. carriers would need. By 2026, every NAIC jurisdiction must have adopted the Model Law on group capital calculation in order to maintain its NAIC accreditation.[3]

2.   Information Sharing Between U.S. Insurance Regulators and Non-U.S. Insurance Regulators

Another important development, begun in 2007 and continuing, resulted from the memoranda of understanding between insurance regulators in various countries, such as the U.K., and various state regulators in the U.S., including those in California, Florida, Massachusetts, New York, Ohio, Pennsylvania, and Washington State. Pursuant to those written understandings, regulators in both the European nations and the state exchange, under specified conditions, otherwise confidential information about persons and entities in the insurance sector of mutual concern.[4]

II.   INSURTECH

The advent of a wholly wired world poses unprecedented challenges to U.S. state insurance regulators, which the NAIC has begun to address through its Innovation Cybersecurity and Technology Committee,[5] and other NAIC committees. The NAIC Center for Insurance Policy and Research has published a series of useful monographs covering the various regulatory considerations inherent in various aspects of insurtech.[6]

---

[3]   https://content.naic.org/cipr-topics/covered-agreement; https://content .naic.org/cmte_e_grp_capital_wg.htm; https://content.naic.org/sites/default/files/ inline-files/440%26450-gcc-combined.pdf (last visited July 12, 2023).

[4]   https://www.iaisweb.org/page/supervisory-material/mmou (last visited July 12, 2023).

[5]   https://content.naic.org/cmte_h.htm (last visited July 12, 2023).

[6]   https://content.naic.org/cipr-topics/insurtech (last visited July 12, 2023).

Some examples of the insurtech challenges confronting regulators include:

- Self-driving cars—what kind of insurance will be needed and for whom? Will the insurance need to cover not only system design and manufacture, but cyberthreats and data breaches?
- Drones which can inspect damaged properties—will drone operators need to be licensed as insurance adjusters?
- Catastrophic weather computer modeling—as insurers increasingly rely on highly complex computer models to measure the risk of hurricanes, earthquakes, tsunamis and other catastrophic weather events, how can regulators understand how the models operate to properly supervise their use in underwriting and rate setting?
- Artificial intelligence in claims handling and other functions—will fair claims handling rules need to adapt?
- Telematics—many states already allow car owners to *voluntarily* agree to have their driving performance continuously monitored which could result in lower auto insurance premiums, but how do regulators ensure that unauthorized invasion of privacy does not occur and that the discounts offered by insurers are fair?
- "Micro-policies—as insurers can underwrite and issue property and casualty policies for particular events with extremely short policy periods, say, only for one day, will state laws requiring 30 days or longer to cancel or non-renew policies need to adapt?
- Health monitoring devices—will life and health insurers and producers be able to offer a health-related smartwatch or a "fit bit" device to policyholders without violating state anti-inducement laws, or will these laws need to be modified, and how can data privacy be maintained? Some states, like New York, have already amended their insurance codes to permit insurers and producers to offer these devices to group health insurance certificate-holders without violating state anti-inducement laws discussed in Chapter 7.[7]
- Automated life insurance underwriting—consumers may well benefit from a dramatic reduction in the time and cost needed to issue policies, but how do regulators ensure that the algorithms and data do not unfairly discriminate, even implicitly, against applicants?

---

[7]   N.Y. Ins. L. §§ 3239, 4224(f).

The NAIC Innovation committee is supposed to coordinate with various other NAIC committees and task forces. *See* https://content.naic.org/cmte-h-collaboration-forum (last visited July 12, 2023). For example, in evaluating the use of artificial intelligence and algorithms by insurers intent on computerizing the underwriting and rating process, the committee plans to work with another newly created NAIC group, the Special Committee on Race and Insurance, to determine if particular regulations are needed to prevent unintentional bias. Regulators in the U.S. have expressed particular concern about insurance companies using algorithms and artificial intelligence to make underwriting decisions and to prescribe policy premium rates. The possibility of unintentional bias against racial minorities and unfair discrimination based on sex stemming from their use has fueled heightened regulatory scrutiny of insurer underwriting and rating practices using this technology.

In 2021 the Colorado Legislature enacted the first statute specifically restricting the use of algorithms, external data and predictive models by insurance companies in underwriting, rating and claims handling.[8] The Colorado law requires the Insurance Commissioner to issue detailed specific regulations after consulting with industry and consumers, and requires insurers to submit detailed explanations of how they are using those tools and the extent to which they have assessed and addressed the risks of fostering implicit biases.

The New York Department of Financial Services issued guidance in 2019 which warned life insurers licensed in New York to be very careful about using technology to speed the underwriting and/or rating process which could lead to unfair discrimination. The Department's Circular Letter No. 1 (2019) stated:

> [T]he use of external data sources, algorithms, and predictive models has a significant potential negative impact on the availability and affordability of life insurance for protected classes of consumers. An insurer should not use an external data source, algorithm or predictive model for underwriting or rating purposes unless the insurer can establish that the data source does not use and is not based in any way on race, color, creed, national origin, status as a victim of domestic violence, past lawful travel, or sexual orientation in any manner, or any other protected class. Moreover, an insurer should also not use an external data source for underwriting or rating purposes unless the use of the external data source is not unfairly discriminatory and complies with all other requirements in the Insurance Law and Insurance Regulations. Second,

---

[8]   Colo. R. S. § 10-3-1104.9.

the use of external data sources is often accompanied by a lack of transparency for consumers. *Where an insurer is using external data sources or predictive models, the reason or reasons for any declination, limitation, rate differential or other adverse underwriting decision provided to the insured or potential insured should include details about all information upon which the insurer based such decision, including the specific source of the information upon which the insurer based its adverse underwriting decision.* (emphasis added)[9]

Given the recency of these various technological innovations there have not been, to date, state court cases or state insurance department enforcement rulings in which insurance companies or insurance professionals have faced regulatory sanctions for employing these technologies. As discussed in Chapter 2, however, there was the decision of the Texas Supreme Court in *Ojo v. Farmers Insurance Group*,[10] which, on remand from the Ninth Circuit Court of Appeals sustained an insurer's use of credit scoring technology as compliant with Texas insurance regulations. That federal appellate court had held that the McCarran-Ferguson Act required deference to state insurance regulation in deciding whether the insurer was violating the federal Fair Housing Act by using technology which produced a disparate impact on minority policyholders, even if there was no evidence that the insurer intended to discriminate on the basis of race or ethnic origin. In the years to come one can reasonably expect state courts and state insurance departments to produce important rulings in this area.

One other aspect of technology which has already generated an insurance regulatory response is the vulnerability of an insurer's IT system to being hacked, to the detriment of policyholders and claimants. As discussed in Chapter 5, led by New York in 2017, currently numerous states have adopted the NAIC Insurer Data Security Model Act requiring licensees to establish and maintain robust defenses against unauthorized computer intrusions. The NAIC Model Act can be accessed here: https://content.naic.org/sites/default/files/inline-files/MDL-668.pdf (last visited July 12, 2023). Moreover, severe regulatory sanctions have already been imposed on insurers which violated state cybersecurity regulations.[11]

---

[9]   https://www.dfs.ny.gov/industry_guidance/circular_letters/cl2019_01 (last visited July 12, 2023).

[10]   356 S.W.3d 421 (Tex. Sup. Ct. 2011).

[11]   https://www.dfs.ny.gov/reports_and_publications/press_releases/pr202105131 (last visited July 12, 2023) (in 2021 two life insurers agreed to pay

Note that New York requires all licensees, including licensed resident *and non-resident* agents, brokers and adjusters, to file annual certifications of compliance with the cybersecurity regulations (except for a licensee employed or retained by, and subject to the same cybersecurity policies and procedures of, another licensee who makes the filing),[12] by contrast, the NAIC Model Act, Section 4, only requires domestic insurers to file annual certifications of compliance with their respective domestic state regulator.

Associated with the problem of preventing data breaches is the phenomenon known as "ransomware" which U.S. insurance regulators have already begun to address. A "ransomware" attack can adversely affect insurance companies in two ways: first, if its own IT system is hacked, and second, if numerous cyber-insurance policyholders file claims for coverage which could lead to massive, unsustainable payouts. The New York Department of Financial Services has published guidance for insurers (and banks) to follow to deter "ransomware" attacks.[13]

Just as improper use of technology can lead to regulatory sanctions, it is also true that technology can aid insurance regulators in assessing the financial health and market conduct of licensees. Blockchain and distributed ledger technology together with "smart contracts" hold the promise of not only improving the efficiency of insurers, reinsurers and producers to the benefit of policyholders and claimants, but also enable regulators to monitor insurance company operations in real time, without the need for more expensive on-site periodic examinations, in a data protected manner. As noted in Chapter 3, states like Kentucky and North Carolina have begun to adopt "regulatory sandbox" laws allowing insurtech companies to flexibly operate on a limited, experimental basis without cumbersome regulation.[14]

Technology can also enhance an insurance company's market conduct by allowing it to quickly respond to the needs of its policyholders. For example, a leading auto insurance company recently touted its telematics

---

$1.8 million penalty to N.Y. Dept. of Fin. Serv. for failing to comply with cybersecurity regulations).

[12]   11 N.Y.C.R.R. Part 500. 17.

[13]   https://www.dfs.ny.gov/industry_guidance/industry_letters/il20210630 _ransomware_guidance (last visited July 12, 2023).

[14]   https://www.insurancejournal.com/news/southeast/2021/10/11/636251 .htm; https://www.insurancejournal.com/news/national/2017/05/16/451177.htm (last visited July 12, 2023).

system not only to effect discounts for safe driving—always with the actual consent of the policyholder who must agree to the telematics system being used—but even to dispatching ambulances and tow trucks to the scene of an accident as soon as a crash is detected by the system and the vehicle operator does not respond to calls.[15]

BOX 9.1 PRACTICAL TIP FOR PRACTITIONERS

Practitioners representing companies whose business models involve technology to underwrite or sell insurance, such as providing necessary software or an electronic platform for the insurer to use —even if they themselves neither underwrite nor sell insurance—should check if a state has set up a "regulatory sandbox" which would allow for waivers of otherwise applicable insurance regulations.[16]

---

[15] https://www.insurancejournal.com/news/national/2023/03/08/711007.htm (last visited July 12, 2023).
[16] *See, e.g,* Kentucky R.S. 304.3-700 et seq; Tit. 8 Vermont Stat. Ann. § 15a; South Dakota Stat. 58-48-1 et seq.

Index